CONVERSATIONS WITH MY FATHER

CONVERSATIONS WITH MY FATHER

Justine Kyle McGrath

HACHETTE
BOOKS
IRELAND

First published in 2014 by Hachette Books Ireland

ISBN: 978 1 444 79735 0

A CIP catalogue record for this title is available from the British Library.

Typeset in AGaramond and Book Bembo by Bookends Publishing Services, Dublin.
Printed and bound by Clays Ltd, St Ives plc

Hachette Books Ireland policy is to use papers that are natural, renewable and
recyclable products and made from wood grown in sustainable forests. The logging
and manufacturing processes are expected to conform to the environmental
regulations of the country of origin.

Hachette Books Ireland
8 Castlecourt Centre
Castleknock
Dublin 15
Ireland

A division of Hachette UK Ltd
338 Euston Road, London NW1 3BH

www.hachette.ie

CONTENTS

To Dad, for believing in me,

and to the Kyle family; past, present and future.

PREFACE

'I believe that what we become depends on what our fathers teach us at odd moments, when they aren't trying to teach us. We are formed by little scraps of wisdom.'
Umberto Eco, *Foucault's Pendulum*

To those who enjoy the game of rugby, particularly those who grew up in the 1940s and 1950s, Jack Kyle is a very familiar name. Up to now, no one has written a book about him and the reasons for this are twofold. Firstly, Dad is quite a private person and for that reason alone always turned down any offers for anyone to write a book about his life or for him to write his memoirs. Secondly, most offers revolved around Dad's life on the rugby pitch, and he feels that would give an unfair slant to his life story. He has always felt that his sporting ability never required a great deal of effort – it came naturally, a gift that nature had bestowed – and so he has always been reluctant to dwell too much on the successes it brought. He always felt that rugby, at the time he was playing, was a recreation – or a re-creation – of yourself; it may give enjoyment but it was not the main part of a player's life.

My paternal grandfather always placed a great emphasis on education, often telling Dad that he was not up at university to learn how to play rugby, but to get his medical degree. He knew that rugby was a very enjoyable part of the university experience for Dad, but was adamant that it was not to interfere with Dad's reason for being there. Dad understood this and put in the effort academically and gained his medical degree, which enabled him to have a very long career as a doctor and a surgeon after his rugby-playing days were over.

When asked in later life whether he was more proud of his OBE or his FRCS (Fellow of the Royal College of Surgeons), Dad said that although he was proud of them both, his FRCS gave him more pleasure because he'd had to work hard to pass the required exams. Whilst also incredibly proud of his OBE (which he was awarded at the end of the 1950s, after his international career was over), it was given for his skills as a rugby player, which he felt had taken less effort on his part.

Dad still loves rugby, although he finds the modern game so changed, compared to when he was playing – for example, there is more emphasis on tackling now rather than running with the ball.

Throughout his life, rugby has given Dad much more than he could ever have hoped for, including many great friends and opportunities to travel, and it has opened doors and provided him with many invitations that he would not have otherwise received.

About two and a half years ago, I came across some pages

of notes Dad had written. When I asked him what they were, he replied they were just some thoughts and memories about his life that he had jotted down. He said it was OK for me to read them and I was immediately struck by the stories in these twenty pages of scribbled notes. I told Dad I would type them up as they would be interesting for the family to have in future years. As I started to do this, it brought up further questions about his life, and this planted the thought in my mind of writing his life story. Initially, it was just a project I decided to work on myself for the family.

I remember the day we first discussed the idea of expanding this project to become a book. Dad lives in Bryansford in County Down, and has a room at the back of the house where he can sit and read and enjoy the beautiful views. We were sitting in this room, enjoying a drink and a chat before dinner about two years ago, looking out at the old stone walls surrounding the farmers' fields, with their alternating herds of cattle and sheep, and with the Mountains of Mourne in the distance. I had already typed up the notes Dad had given me, but he had not yet thought of turning it into a book. Dad was nearing his eighty-seventh birthday and started talking about his good fortune at having led such an interesting life, and then he said that he now felt if we could work on a book together – and if I would write his life story as he wanted it told – then he would consider putting it out to a wider audience.

During our initial conversations about what should be in

the book, I became aware there were a lot of things about Dad's life I had yet to discover and many areas about which I knew very little. However, this wasn't a new experience for me. In 1991, Dad was awarded an honorary degree at Queen's University and, as I listened to the citation being read, I began to wonder who this person was they were talking about. I didn't know about the many awards he had received, both for his rugby and his medical career, or about the real extent of his rugby prowess. I hadn't realised just how much he was admired, not just as a former rugby player, but as a surgeon, who had left his own country to work in Central Africa.

I said to Dad after the ceremony, *'I realised today that, in some ways, I don't really know you at all.'*

He laughed out loud and remarked on the truth that most children have no thoughts about what their parents' lives were like before they arrived!

This book evolved naturally through a series of conversations held over the course of a year or so, where I would ask Dad about a particular time in his life and would then let him reminisce and tell me as much as he could remember. I owe Dad a lot for entrusting me to tell his life story. I know there are others who may have done a better job, but none who enjoys the close relationship we have.

I am thrilled that after so many hours of talking and revisiting memories through photo albums, scrapbooks and letters, Dad has been able to share an account of a life rich in many varied experiences – an account that can be enjoyed beyond those of us in his immediate family.

Naturally enough, this book includes tales from the world of sport, but also collates Dad's life in medicine, his travels and his love of literature, as well as accounts of some of the fascinating people he has met. Dad has always been a great reader and loves to quote poetry (most of which he has memorised), so his story would not be complete without including some of his favourite poems, as it is one of his great passions. He often says that this was the triumph of memory over creativity or originality; nevertheless it has given him much pleasure over the years.

Because Dad played rugby over fifty years ago, I have wondered how many people would remember him from his rugby-playing days. Then a moment of serendipity occurred when I was in his study looking through some old articles and came across one from the *Belfast Telegraph*. As I picked it up and read it – it was written by Alf McCreary in 1991 – it echoed my own thoughts exactly.

Earlier this year Jack Kyle, the legendary rugby player who helped Ireland win the Grand Slam in 1948 and Triple Crown in 1949 and the Championship in 1951, was back in Belfast. He was receiving an Honorary Degree from Queen's University for his commitment and service to the underprivileged of Central Africa, and deservedly so. It was a dignified and moving ceremony, and, as the citation was delivered by a senior academic at Queen's, Jack Kyle's remarkable achievements were regaled to a packed Sir William Whitla Hall which included hundreds of young people and their friends.

Even though Kyle achieved national rugby fame many years ago, his story has a challenging and an endearing freshness – the man who turned his back on fame and devoted his medical skills to the underprivileged in the Third World has a tale worth telling to every generation.

It is true that if you write about Jack Kyle from a rugby angle, the audience might be narrowed down not only in age but in range of interest. The exploits of even the most remarkable rugby players like Kyle may even bore those who have no interest in this sport; but Jack Kyle's story, in the hands of a good feature writer or reporter who understands that this man's worth and example rises far above the mere sports field, could hardly fail to impress or inspire people of all ages.

Being the daughter of Jack Kyle has had no downsides for me whatsoever. I consider myself so lucky to have been born the daughter of such a remarkable man.

My father's legacy will be his rugby and his medical work, but I know that he will also be remembered as a decent man, and if decency were measured in stars then, to me, he is a galaxy.

Justine Kyle McGrath
July 2014

CHAPTER ONE

AN ULSTER CHILDHOOD

'There is always one moment in childhood
when the door opens and lets the future in.'
Graham Greene

We began the 'discussions proper' about Dad's life on a
bitterly cold morning towards the end of January 2013, as
we sat in his lounge with hot mugs of tea. Dad's garden
was picture-postcard perfect – a winter wonderland with
everything covered in a blanket of snow. The stream in
the front garden was frozen solid and the bridge spanning
it was entirely white. Whilst our eyes were continually
drawn to the snowfall outside, I was also listening to Dad's
lovely Irish brogue as he transported me back to the 1930s

and a whole different world. Dad's childhood seemed the easiest – if obvious – place to start his story.

Dad's full name is John Wilson Kyle, named after his father, and he was born on 10 February 1926. This date has provided the family with some amusement, not to mention a little frustration, over the years because, at some point, by some journalist, it was incorrectly published as 10 January 1926. Despite contacting many publications, some refused to believe us or to change it, and it remains incorrectly published in the majority of books, newspapers and articles in which Dad is mentioned. We've given up trying to persuade people that we may know better, so I am happy to have the opportunity to right that wrong here.

During my childhood, I was not particularly interested in my family history, but as an adult it has become a great interest. As my father talked about his parents and grandparents, I heard echoes of other family members and noticed resemblances in photographs, and my thirst to know more continued unabated.

I did find out some very interesting information about Dad's great-grandfather quite by chance. My cousin's neighbour is a genealogist and shared a booklet with my cousin entitled *A Generation of Montgomerys* written by the Right Reverend Bishop Henry Montgomery, the father of Field Marshal Montgomery of Alamein. It included a reference to a John Wilson, who it turned out is my father's great-grandfather.

There are several references in the booklet to Dad's great-grandfather, who was born in 1815 and worked as a coachman for the Reverend Samuel Montgomery at Ballynascreen Rectory, located in Draperstown in County Derry. The one below gives an insight into the type of person Dad's great-grandfather was:

Perhaps John Wilson, the coachman, was the greatest character. He was a typical Irishman, with a great deal of black hair, a florid complexion and blue eyes and he stood over six feet in height. If the truth were spoken, I think we boys looked forward to Wilson's society in the harness room as much as to anything else going on in Ballynascreen. We spent whole afternoons there laughing at his jokes.

The booklet goes on to say that John Wilson was devoted to his master, and the feeling seemed to be mutual, as we are told he was with the family for many years and was seen as an integral part of it.

So, it appears that Dad's father was named after his own grandfather and that Dad has the same name as his father and his great-grandfather. No wonder I was confused when doing the family tree!

Having gone that far back, I asked Dad about his own grandparents, whom he does remember.

❀

'Well, Grandfather Kyle was called Joseph and he was born in 1850. He was a baker, but used to call himself a 'master baker'. He married Elizabeth Wilson. They both came from the area around Draperstown in County Derry. I remember visiting my great-grandfather's grave [the aforementioned John Wilson] there when I was young. We also used to visit my father's aunt, Lucy Wilson, who lived in the Gate Lodge of the Clarkes of Upperlands near Maghera, County Derry. I remember my grandparents quite well – Grandmother Kyle was born in 1850 and died in 1934 at the age of eighty-four, and Grandfather Kyle died in 1936, at the age of eighty-six. I remember my grandfather as a kind but firm man who smoked a pipe, and who went down to the local post office every Friday to collect his pension of ten shillings.

'One of my most vivid memories is of me and my older brother Eric going into our grandfather's room and

Me (on the left), Grandfather Kyle and Eric, about 1932.

jumping on the bed, saying, "Tell us a story about Tarzan." He usually obliged, happy to make up stories to keep two small boys amused.

'Grandfather Kyle had twelve siblings, nine boys and three girls. Nine of them emigrated to America in the aftermath of the famines of the 1840s, when life in Ireland was desperately hard. Over two million people died during the potato famine and thousands left Ireland. What I find incredibly poignant is that Grandfather Kyle never heard from any of his nine siblings again, although I was told by my father that one of my grandfather's sisters became matron of the Massachusetts General Hospital in Boston.

'It is hard to imagine such suffering and incredible to think that those living only two generations back from me had to endure such a horrific ordeal. To think that we don't even know for sure whether all of my grandfather's nine siblings arrived safely in America is so sad. I've often wondered why they did not keep in contact. My only explanation is that mail then was very unreliable and it took so long, by the time a letter was sent and received, the relative had moved to another area. I am not sure how my grandfather felt about not seeing any of his siblings again, as he never mentioned it.

'Many who were forced to leave Ireland often thought nostalgically about the country they had left behind, and there were many songs extolling the beauty of Ireland and the sadness at having to leave it. Songs such as 'The

Old Bog Road', 'The Hills of Donegal' and 'Galway Bay', which my father enjoyed very much.

'In 1973, I did a surgical course in Boston for three weeks and decided to try and see if there was any truth in the rumour regarding my grandfather's sister becoming matron of the Massachusetts General Hospital. When I asked at the hospital, though, I was told that records only went back to 1923, so no one knew if a Kyle had been a matron there before that. Thinking there would only be a few Kyles in the phonebook, I decided it was worthwhile ringing a few of them to see if I could find out any information about my relatives. I was more than a little put out when I opened the phone directory to find hundreds of Kyles listed, so that put an end to my search for any family connections. It's funny because people often remarked that I bore a very close resemblance to Danny Kaye – the famous actor of the 1950s and 1960s – and if you look at his photograph, there is a certain resemblance! I also used to listen to an excellent African-American jazz pianist called Billy Kyle who played with Louis Armstrong, now there's someone I wish I could have been related to!

'My grandparents on my mother's side were named Warren. We just knew them as Granny and Granddad Warren, although I do know my Granny Warren was called Isabella. I remember my grandfather being an avid reader and there were always a lot of books in their house. Granny Warren used to visit our home once a week and she would bake soda bread, apple bread, potato bread and lots of other delicious treats. She was a very energetic woman, as I recall. I know that Granddad Warren died when he was sixty-four and that, in later life, Granny Warren lived with her daughter Mabel in Limavady. That's about all I remember about them.

'My father married Elizabeth Warren in early 1924. She was from Belfast and her family lived off the Crumlin Road. She had three sisters – Ria, Mabel and Cathleen – and two brothers – Eric and Norman. My mother was born in 1905, so she was only nineteen when she married my father, who was forty-one at the time, so there was quite a big age gap, but that was quite common in those days and no one thought anything at all about it.'

My parents on their wedding day, 1924.

'So, tell me more about your father,' I ask. 'He was quite the businessman from what I remember you saying?'

'Yes, he was. He was an only child, born in June 1883, and in the 1920s, was the Irish manager of the North British Rubber Company whose headquarters were in Edinburgh. He met my mother when she was working as a secretary in the same company. His job was to manage the supply of all types of rubber goods to other companies and shops. The offices and warehouse were situated in Chichester Street in Belfast, beside the old Plaza, which was a venue for shows and dances.

'During the war years [1939–1945], the Germans invented a magnetic mine. If a ship came close to one of these mines, the mine was drawn towards the ship and then exploded. So it became necessary to develop a method of demagnetising ships. This was called 'degaussing' and consisted of a ring of wires around the ship. These wires had to be protected from the sea and my father was approached to find a way to cover them. A rubber solution was developed with his help – at one time, my father had over a hundred men working on the degaussing of the ships in Harland and Wolff.

'Such was the success of the degaussing in Belfast, that the North British Rubber Company asked him to take over the degaussing in Glasgow, but as he had a young family of five children at the time, four of whom were at school, he turned down the offer. My father was a very committed family man and we always came first.

'During the Second World War when my father was going to Harland and Wolff to see how the degaussing was progressing, he would take me and my brother Eric. It was very exciting for us to be allowed to walk the decks of these huge ships.'

'That reminds me of the time we went on the SA Vaal *when Caleb [my brother] and I were young,' I said. 'Do you remember? I remember being amazed at the size of the ship.'*

'That's right. It was 1978 when we travelled from Cape Town to Southampton. I remember taking you and Caleb to Stuttafords, a department store in Cape Town, to get fancy dress outfits. I knew there may be a fancy dress party and no way was I going to be caught out. If I remember rightly, you chose a nurse's uniform and Caleb chose an army outfit. Once when I was young and your mother

My brother Eric, myself and my sister Betty, at Aunt Lucy's, near Maghera in County Derry, about 1930.

and I went to a fancy dress party, I put a broom across my shoulders, put on an old checked shirt and covered myself in straw and went as a scarecrow! I won a prize for that outfit, but I wasn't prepared to have to think up and make outfits for you two on my holiday!

'Getting back to the family, my brother Eric was the first born in 1924. I followed in 1926 and then my three sisters came along – Betty in 1928, Brenda in 1934 and then there was a seven-year gap before Beatrice was born in 1941. The 'three Bs' as you and Caleb call them. We were all born at home except for Beatrice, as was the custom at the time. There was also another child who died at birth, I believe my father wanted to call him Louis.

'Northern Ireland at this time was relatively settled, unlike the Republic, which was still dealing with the after-effects of the Civil War in 1922. I was born into a divided

Dad, me and Mum, holding Brenda, with Betty and Eric sat in front.

Beatrice with our dog, around 1950.

Ireland and, like most people, feel that the history of Ireland is a tragic one. Although Northern Ireland was attempting to build up its economy in the late 1920s, and did have the advantage of being able to trade with Britain, it also hit a worldwide recession after the Wall Street Crash of 1929.

'Home was Kinnaird Street on the Antrim Road in Belfast. I was born when my mother was twenty.'

'So your mother had given birth twice before she was twenty-one! She was so young, I just cannot imagine having such a large family and being so young, but I suppose at least she had the energy to cope with all of you!'

'Well, not only did she have her children to deal with, but she also had my father's parents living with them. As social benefits were quite meagre in those days, many adults supported their own parents by having them live with them, so it was a very full house with four children and four adults – by the time Beatrice was born, my grandparents had both died.

'When I was around seven years old, we moved to

Glenburn Park off the Old Westland Road in North Belfast. The house was a large, detached, three-storey building that had been built about the beginning of the 1900s. There was a study on the first floor, four bedrooms on the second floor and it also had two large attic rooms on the top floor. Many of the rooms had beautiful big fireplaces. The garden had a lawn the size of a tennis court along the side of the house, which was adorned with many flowerbeds, one of which contained roses.

'Some years back, the family were rather surprised to discover that my father had been married when he was younger and that his first wife had given birth to a daughter. Tragically, his wife died in childbirth and I believe their daughter was brought up by his wife's family. My mother knew that her husband had a child from a previous marriage and she visited his daughter's family on occasion. Your Aunty Betty has also told me that she can remember going a few times with our father to visit his daughter.

'Although my father was not a religious person in the strict sense of the word, he felt that religion was an important part of life and therefore we were taught to say our prayers. We had grace before meals and sometimes had Bible readings. We were encouraged to go to Sunday school and the family attended, en masse, the Fort William Presbyterian Church in the days of the Reverend Harrison and the Reverend Breakey.

Myself and Brenda in the garden of our house, 1935.

'We were all quite good at sports, but I don't recall my parents being especially sporty – although I do remember my mother winning the Mother's Race at the school sports day! Sport, however, definitely ran in our genes. My sister Betty showed great talent for hockey and played for Ulster Senior Ladies when she was still at school. After that, she went on to captain the Irish ladies hockey side and was captain when the team won the Triple Crown in 1950. She was a very talented sportswoman and enjoyed playing hockey so much that she went on to become a PE teacher.

'Brenda was also a talented hockey player and, although she never got an international cap for Ireland, she travelled with the Irish ladies hockey side to Australia to play in the World Cup in 1956. My youngest sister Beatrice, who is fifteen years younger than me, grew up surrounded by all her siblings playing sport and, although she was also very talented, she never showed an interest in playing sport to any degree – she was probably fed up listening to the sporting achievements of her brothers and sisters. People often asked Beatrice if she was going to be as good a hockey player as her sisters. The pressure to be good at something just because your father, mother or siblings happen to be is very unfair.'

I know what Dad means. Whilst my brother Caleb and I both enjoyed our sport, we weren't naturally gifted to the extent Dad was, and we both felt the pressure of 'being a Kyle' – though I suspect it was a lot worse for Caleb. He enjoyed rugby, but after injuring his neck, he had to give it up. Dad always felt it was important that we were given the freedom to develop the talents and interests we had, and he never put any pressure on us to play sport unless we enjoyed it – and he never expected us to shine just because he was our father. Dad felt it was very hard on someone to be talked about as 'so and so's sister or brother, husband or wife or son or daughter' and he always felt it was important

My parents and my sister Beatrice in Portrush, about 1940.

In the sea with Eric and my father, about 1930 (I'm on the right).

for someone to be acknowledged as an individual in their own right, something for which I am very grateful.

'Tell me some more about your childhood.'

'During our childhood, in the summers, my father would rent a house in Whitehead, Portstewart or Portrush, where we enjoyed swimming and learned to dive – we even took part in diving exhibitions for charity organisations, like the lifeboats. We also took part in lots of other outdoor activities, such as rounders, cricket and football. We sometimes went to Tyrella Beach near Newcastle, County Down. My father always encouraged races up and down the beach and I think this is where we developed a healthy competition and love of games and sport, which were to become such a huge part of all of our lives. Weekends were also a source of adventure, and my father and mother would pack up all the paraphernalia required for outings and the five of us kids would squeeze

Dad with me, Betty and Eric. We used to go on many trips out in the car.

into the back of the car and head off for picnics at different places, such as the River Roe at Limavady, where Eric and I learned to fish. We would often bring back some trout for my mother to cook on the primus stove for a good lunch. Often on a Sunday or at the weekend, my father would take us for drives in the car and I remember often stopping for an ice-cream at Capronis in Bangor.

'It was all much simpler than today, but we had lots of fun. My parents had a very strong union and our welfare as children was their main concern. My mother was a quiet, gentle woman who kept the home fires burning, and the family well fed and nurtured. My parents went to the cinema once a week and I also remember them enjoying themselves listening to music on the old gramophone – such as the records of John McCormack and Gracie Fields – and we all loved the song of the 'Laughing Policeman'.

'Although there was plenty of fun to be had, my father did enforce discipline and expected us to behave properly. He would not tolerate tantrums and we would not have dreamed of answering back or being cheeky or rude – but he also had a very good sense of humour. I remember when my brother and I had reached a certain age and he felt we should be told the facts of life. It was not a task he relished, so he kept it very straightforward and simple. I also remember him saying to Eric and me, "Now, boys, there will come a time when you will meet girls and you will think of getting married, and it is very important that you don't just marry a girl because she is good looking or has a good figure, as that could be a disaster – but if you can get that thrown in, all the better – of course, I was very fortunate with your mother!"

'My father didn't swear, and so I can clearly remember a joke he told Eric and me which was the one and only time I ever heard him swear. The joke goes that a minister came up to his church one day and found the verger clearing up the area around the church where there were many pigeons. The verger was saying, "Shoo, shoo, bugger off" to the dirty birds. The minister said, "My good man, do you realise that you are practically on holy ground? What would the members of the congregation think if they heard you using such language? I will tell you what you need to say to the pigeons. You just say, 'Shoo, shoo, shoo, shoo', and the pigeons will bugger off themselves!"'

'*That wouldn't even be considered swearing in today's language!*' I said.

'That just goes to show how much times have changed, but I have always hated a lot of swearing and I think that it was instilled in us from an early age. When I think of my father, I always think of the lines from the poem called 'Father and Son' by F.R. Higgins which he loved:

> *For that proud wayward man, now my heart breaks*
> *Breaks for that man whose mind was a secret eyrie,*
> *Whose kind hand was sole signet of his race,*
> *Who curbed me, scorned my green ways, yet increasingly*
> *loved me*
> *Till death drew its grey blind down his face.*

'My father had his first heart attack in 1948. The treatment in those days was to get into bed and stay there for three months and not to move. The logic behind it was to rest the heart. My father, being a very active man, found this very difficult. He did recover from it – though at one stage we were not too sure he would – and survived for another six years. He died in 1954 from another heart attack and a stroke. Sadly, my mother died nine months later in 1955. At the time, we thought she had died as a result of kidney failure, but I found out many years later that she died from what is known as an iatrogenic disease, which happens when you are made worse by something that is meant to cure you. The great Frank Pantridge, who I will

Myself and my parents enjoying one of our many trips to the seaside, around 1932.

tell you more about later, told me they did not know it at the time, but that she died as a result of the injections she was being given for her rheumatoid arthritis. She was only fifty when she died.'

'Oh my goodness, she was so young, that is so sad. I can't believe I didn't know that until now.'

'It was very hard on Beatrice because she was still at school at the time, so Eric and I did all we could to look after her, until she was eighteen.'

Having listened to Dad talk at length about his family, I am struck by what a simple, happy childhood he had and also by what a united family they were. As Dad said, in many ways, life was more straightforward then, and roles were very clear-cut.

The close bond Dad and his siblings had as children still exists today and, as a family, we are all very close. My grandparents must have played a role in that, for which I am grateful, as, growing up, I witnessed what it meant to be part of a large, loving, extended family.

CHAPTER TWO

THE IMPORTANCE
OF EDUCATION

'Education is not the filling of a pail,
but the lighting of a fire.'
W.B. Yeats

I would travel up to Bryansford at least once a month to
visit Dad, but when we were working on this book, the
visits had an added purpose. One Friday afternoon, as I
drove the road that leads from Hilltown to Bryansford,
where the spectacular views of the Mountains of Mourne
always relax me, I thought about what we should discuss.
As we had started with his childhood, it seemed natural to
follow on chronologically and ask Dad about his time at
school and his education.

❁

'I was enrolled at Belfast Royal Academy [BRA] in 1930 at the very young age of four. I wasn't a brilliant student, but I managed, with a certain amount of perseverance, to get through my exams. I loved school though and all that went with it, including all the sports we were able to play. I never missed a day of school in the whole time I was there – it may be hard to believe, but it's absolutely true. However, I was also a bit of a dreamer, which is not conducive to concentrated studies. In those days, the two important school exams were known as the Junior Certificate and Senior Certificate, and you took them at the ages of fifteen or sixteen and seventeen or eighteen respectively. BRA was a co-ed school and that certainly added an extra interest to my time there!

'There was a synagogue near the school in the north part of Belfast, and I went to school with many people from the Jewish community. I had a good relationship with the Jewish students, whom I found to be very intelligent with a great capacity for friendship. I always found it very difficult to understand the anti-Semitism I saw in the wider world at the time, especially in Germany.

'About ten years ago, Israel Schachter, who was in my year at school, returned to Belfast to present a portrait of his own father, who had been the Chief Rabbi in Belfast from the mid-1920s to the early 1950s. The portrait was painted by Taylor Carson and was presented to the Belfast

The Belfast Royal Academy, where I spent fourteen years, starting in 1930 at the age of four.

Museum. I attended the ceremony and was delighted to reconnect with an old school friend.

'Rugby was not the only sport that I played. I also played cricket at school, captaining the First XI, and was also chosen to play for Ulster Schools in Dublin and in Belfast. I also won the Athletics Cup at the school sports day and held the school's record for the long jump for many years.'

As we talked about his school days, Dad told me how he started playing rugby.

'Alec Foster, who was the headmaster in my early years, was himself a rugby player. He had played and captained Ireland in 1910, 1911 and 1912 and had also toured with the Lions to South Africa in 1910. He encouraged rugby at the academy and I benefited from this greatly. We became friends in later years after I'd left school. He was a very intelligent man and a great headmaster who took a keen interest in his pupils and their welfare. Even as schoolchildren, we recognised that he was a remarkable man. He was a classical scholar and had graduated first in his year from Queen's University. One of the benefits of his headship was the purchase of Castle Grounds on the Antrim Road, a beautifully situated place below Cave Hill with views over Belfast Lough. A plaque at the Castle Grounds commemorates the foresight of Alec Foster, along with another man, Lord Justice Babbington, who both realised how important sport was in the all-round development of the pupils.

'I loved all sports and played any and every sport I could. I remember the first time I played rugby. The coach ordered me into the scrum but I hated the aggressive contact nature of the position I was in. After that game, I decided that the scrum was the last place in the world I ever intended to be again, so I asked the coach if I could play at full-back. Luckily, he agreed, and I played in that position up to my first year in the First XV at school. Then one day, the sports master, Mr Stewart, moved me to out-half. I honestly don't know why he did, perhaps he just wanted to try me in that position, but I stayed there for the rest of my rugby-playing career. I was very fortunate to be moved to out-half as the position clearly suited my abilities, as I had a quick burst of speed over a short distance. Although the position was mainly called out-half, it was also known by other names, such as fly-half and the now-obsolete first five-eighths.'

Dad's talent for rugby was quickly noticed and he was selected to captain the First XV and was chosen to play for

Ulster School Boys against Leinster in Dublin in 1943 and in Belfast in 1944. He never envisaged the future successes that would occur at Lansdowne Road when he first visited Dublin in 1943 for that inter-provincial match. He recalls how thrilled he felt when, at the tender age of seventeen, he was selected to play for Ulster School Boys.

'I remember reading books about Dublin in anticipation of the trip, and learning about Trinity College, the *Book of Kells* and everything about this great city that seemed a world away from Belfast. It was a thrill to be travelling the hundred or so miles to Dublin and to play in Ireland's international ground – I'm pleased to say the rugby went well too and we won the match 16–3. We returned to Belfast on the train that evening. It never entered my thoughts that one day I would wear the green jersey for Ireland, be on a Grand Slam team, tour with the Lions and play with the Barbarians.

'My brother Eric and I played rugby, cricket and we even boxed up to the age of about fourteen, but my father put a stop to that, much to the annoyance of the boxing coach who felt that we had some talent that could have been nurtured and taken forward. My father was very protective of us and also wise enough to understand the medical implications in later life of receiving continuous blows to the head. He knew it would never be a full-time competitive sport for either of us, so it seemed prudent to withdraw us from the sport before any brain damage was done.

*Playing rugby for BRA. I'm stood in the second row, fourth from the left.
My brother Eric is seated in front of me, second from the right. Mr Stewart,
who first told me to play at out-half, is standing on the right.*

'Eric received his share of the sporting plaudits too. He captained the school First XI at cricket, played scrum-half for the First XV and, in later years, played scrum-half for what was then North Rugby Club, now Belfast Harlequins. He also played rugby for Ulster and got an Irish trial, but never received an international cap. His death in 1990 from a heart attack still saddens me.'

Dad talks about his older brother with such fondness, and stops for a moment to remember him. I can remember the time around Uncle Eric's death very well. It was

Myself (in front) and Eric on a family trip to the seaside.
Notice the rope around me – I always had to be 'the horse'!

the first time I had seen Dad cry and, similar to most children, the sight came as a bit of a shock, though I wasn't surprised by the depth of emotion his brother's death had caused.

Returning to our conversation, I wondered if Uncle Eric had found it hard to see Dad's success as a rugby player.

'I don't believe so. Eric was never ever jealous or resentful of my success as a rugby player. As brothers, we were very close and shared a love of so many other things – jazz music, sport and good books and films. I miss him deeply.'

I also miss my Uncle Eric. Every time I saw him, he would have a huge smile on his face and a story to tell. He also had a huge, deep belly laugh that made you happy just to hear it. I don't think I ever saw him complain or grumble and life was a lot of fun when he was around.

Dad goes on to tell me about his final days at school.

'In my final year at school, I was made head boy. I was honoured to be given this position and I didn't find it difficult in any way. I still wasn't sure what career I wanted at that stage, but that was about to change.'

'So how did you come to the decision to study medicine? I mean you left it quite late, if you were only deciding in your final year at school.'

'Well, there were no career guidance counsellors in schools in those days and there was an assumption that I would go into business with my father. However, my father knew that I had neither the interest nor the skill required for a career in business – he used to say to me, "If you were to make your way in the world of business, you'd starve!" With this in mind, and knowing me as well as he did, he maintained that I needed to be in a job where people came to me rather than me having to sell my services to them. One day out of the blue when we were driving somewhere, he said, "Have you ever thought about doing medicine?" I replied that I hadn't, to which he simply said, "Think about it."

'Well, I duly did and I never could have imagined the career path and the sort of life it was going to give me – travel to foreign climes and the opportunity to fulfil my potential and to do a job I loved. I often think back to that very short conversation with my father and feel so grateful he knew me as well as he did. He also knew that I needed a bit of encouragement and a push now and again. He would say to me, "You'd be dead if only you had the sense to stiffen!"'

I never knew my grandfather, but from everything that Dad tells me about him, I wish I had. He seemed to have known instinctively what was right for his children. Although he seemed quite the disciplinarian, there was clearly a huge amount of love in the family and I still find it incredibly touching how close my father is to all his siblings.

Dad has been a lifelong learner. He has a study where there are hundreds of books of all types – poetry, novels, philosophy, religion, biography, travel, sport and medicine. Until recently, he attended surgical meetings, over ten years after his retirement, to keep up with the advances in medicine. He also continues to teach himself French and he still reads a prolific amount.

For Caleb and me, his love of education has resulted in a lot more than just wanting us to pass exams. He passed on the importance of fulfilling your potential and always said to us: 'Get what you like or you learn to like what you get.' Perseverance was another quality he instilled in us. When we failed an exam, he would always tell us to try again. He got this from his own father, who would say to Dad, when he failed an exam, 'Well, you gave it a terrible fright and you will definitely get it the next time.' Even though he was not an A-grade student, Dad persevered in order to reach his goal of becoming a surgeon.

Dad has given me a love of reading for which I will always be thankful, and as I get older I am even beginning to appreciate much of the poetry that he has been quoting to me all my life and which used to have me rolling my eyes in exasperation. Oh, how I wish I had taken more of it in, but I guess we come to different bits of knowledge in our own way and in our own time. Given that Dad would have been at school during the Second World War, I am fascinated to know what it was like being a teenager at such a momentous time in history.

'It's interesting but often, at the time, you don't understand or know the significance of what you are living through. Of course, we were well aware that it was very serious, but life had to go on whether you liked it or not. My father had built an air raid shelter in our back garden, which the neighbours initially laughed at, but were only too happy to use when they needed it.

'The worst of the bombings in Belfast took place on the night of 15 April 1941 when 900 people were killed and roughly 10,000 were made homeless. Belfast suffered a huge number of casualties during the war, more than any other UK city except London. After the first raids on Belfast, it was decided to evacuate the students from Belfast Royal Academy to Coleraine and Portrush. I think we were to be sent to the Northern Counties Hotel in Portrush, but many parents decided not to send their children there, including mine, so BRA remained open. I carried on going to school all through the war.

'One of the tasks senior pupils were given during the war was fire-watching duties and I did that on several occasions. This involved checking that there was nothing on fire in the school as a result of raids by German bombers. Fortunately. there never was and we escaped unscathed.

'In April 1941, during the worst raids in Belfast, my father arranged for us to go to Templepatrick every evening after dinner, where we stayed in a boarding house, and he brought us back for school the next morning. We did that for several months. During the first big raid on Belfast, we happened to be visiting my father's cousin Billy Cooke and his wife Sheila in Enniskillen. I don't remember us having to spend any length of time in the air-raid shelter in the garden and we just carried on with life as best we could. I do remember the lists and lists of names in the *Belfast Telegraph* of the young men who had been killed in action. So many families were left devastated, it was incredibly tragic.

'I finished school after sitting my Senior Certificate in June 1944. I wasn't unduly worried about most of the exams, but I do remember worrying about physics and Latin, which I found much more difficult – and I was right to be concerned, as I ended up having to resit them before I could go to university!'

CHAPTER THREE

LIFE AT UNIVERSITY

'This isn't so much a question of intelligence as it is of perseverance.'
Peter Gormley, fellow medical graduate,
to Dad when they were studying for exams

Dad always used to disagree with the old saying that school days are the best days of your life. He maintained that the best days of your life are those you spend at university, because you have the freedom to live your life on your own terms for the first time, whilst studying for a career and with plenty of enjoyment thrown in as well. He strongly encouraged both Caleb and me to go to university.

I imagine times were very different at university

when Dad enrolled and I was interested to hear how he found being thrown into studying medicine, having only recently decided to become a doctor.

❀

'I coped academically, but I had to work hard to pass exams and had to persevere on several occasions when I found I was perhaps falling behind with a subject. Entry into Queen's University came after a couple of challenges, namely that I had to resit physics and Latin – you had to pass both subjects to do medicine in those days. As mentioned, I left school in June 1944 and started life at Queen's the following October, though I continued to live at home and travelled in and out by bus every day.

'There were a hundred students studying medicine in my first year, of whom only twenty were women, quite different from today where there are about 280 students studying the course each year, and up to 70 per cent of them are women!

'The subjects we studied in the first year were physics, chemistry, botany and zoology. I remember a zoology practical that year when we had to dissect a dogfish, a rabbit and a frog. Fortunately, I wasn't squeamish and found the whole process very interesting. The zoology professor was T. Thompson Flynn – Errol Flynn's father. I thought he was a very kind man. He made the lectures very interesting and often mentioned his son, of whom he was very proud. He told us that he went to see all his films, sometimes more than once.

'I got through first year without too much difficulty, although I still struggled with physics, which I had to repeat. In my second year, I studied anatomy, physiology and biochemistry, and, again, there was a lot of work involved, as you might expect. My main challenge was memorising the parts of the body for anatomy. In fact, the memory work needed for anatomy was like learning off the phone book, there were so many different bones, muscles and body parts that we had to ensure we knew. During those first two years, most of the work we undertook was theory-based and we were confined to the university, then, during third year, we started the practical side of our studies and the real work of becoming a doctor began.

'The main part of the practical work took place at the Royal Victoria Hospital in Belfast, which, along with the City Hospital, was the main hospital in the city. We were also sent to the City Hospital and the Benn Hospital in Belfast, for training in eye, ear, nose and throat problems, and the Royal Maternity Hospital, which was actually part of the Royal Victoria.

'The Royal, as it was commonly known, was designed in 1899 and had one long corridor with twenty wards leading off it, which were built right beside each other with no space in between them and some of the wards had balconies at the end of them. Of course it has been

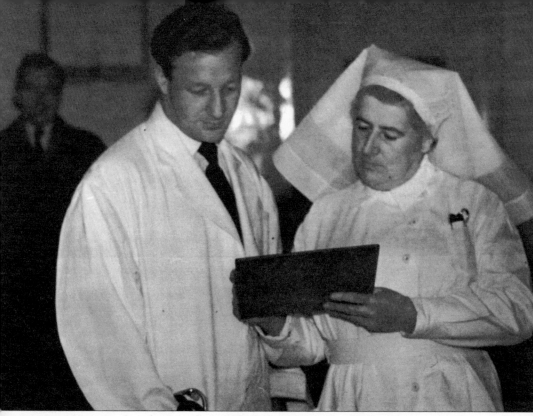

Learning to be a doctor at the Royal Victoria Hospital in Belfast, about 1948.

completely renovated since I started there. There also used to be tennis courts at the back of the hospital building where we sometimes used to play after a day's work.

'The experience of working the wards, with lecture rounds and clinics, provided plenty of stimulation and, in those days, students lived for a month in the hospital and were attached to a ward, which could be either medical or surgical.

'I was attached to two surgical wards – 19 and 20, under the doyenne of surgeon Barney Purce – and also to two medical wards – 7 and 8, under Dr Boyd Campbell. Barney Purce was another quite remarkable man who performed a lot of the chest surgeries at the hospital. But because Cecil

Calvert, who was the neurosurgeon, had been called to Oxford towards the end of the war to attend to head and brain injuries, Barney Purce took over the brain surgery cases at the Royal as well. Back in the late 1930s, he had operated on a malignant melanoma on my father's ankle and also removed some glands in his groin to make sure the melanoma hadn't spread.

'I passed all my exams in my third, fourth and final years at Queen's, despite my six months away with the British and Irish Lions, which I don't think harmed my studies at all – the break was so enjoyable, I came back fully prepared to get my head down and study more.

I graduated in medicine in June 1951. So I was then able to use the letters MB (Bachelor of Medicine) BCh (Bachelor of Surgery) and BAO (Bachelor of the Art of Obstetrics) after my name. It was a very proud day for me, because my parents were both able to attend my graduation. My father had been ill, having suffered his heart attack three years earlier. There had been no doctors in either of my parents' families, so I think they were quite proud to have one son graduating as a doctor, and a bit relieved that I had made it! It was a wonderful day for me – one that I can still remember sixty-three years later.

'I received my diploma in the Whitla Hall in Queen's, from the chancellor of the university who, at that time, was the highly regarded Field Marshal Lord Alanbrooke, who had been the Chief of the Imperial General Staff

Graduating from Queen's University, 1951.

during the war. He had played a very significant role in the war and it was quite an honour to be handed your degree scroll from such a man.

'After graduating from Queen's, I was appointed as a house surgeon at the Royal Victoria where I gained experience by spending three months in the surgical ward in the fracture clinic, run by Mr Withers and Bob Wilson, and three months in a medical ward under Dr Boyd Campbell. This was followed by another three-month stint in a surgical ward under Professor Rogers and Sinclair Irwin, and the final three months of the year were spent under the tutelage of Mr Wheeler and Kennedy Hunter in eye, ear, nose and throat. I enjoyed all my surgical training and was very grateful to all the various teachers I had along the way.

'At the end of that year with the idea of finally specialising in surgery, I applied and was accepted for the job of Senior House Surgeon at the Royal, which I did for six months. This required me to do surgery in the outpatients clinic, and included tasks such as suturing, taking care of varicose veins and opening abscesses. Although not particularly exciting, it was all part of the necessary first steps on the road to becoming a surgeon.

'Looking back on it, it is amazing how much medicine has changed during my lifetime. When I started practising, an abscess had to be opened and when patients required an anaesthetic, they were put on a table and a large strap was put across them. There was no anaesthetist and the medical student was told to put the nitrous oxide up to nine or ten to put the patient to sleep. This may seem somewhat barbaric with today's sophisticated anaesthetics, but it was considered quite normal then and nobody knew any differently.

'In order to pursue surgery, I obtained a part-time lectureship in the Anatomy Department of Queen's. I wanted to do this, as I knew it would be of help to me in my future exams to become a Fellow of the Royal College of Surgeons. Following my time there, I worked as a Senior House Surgeon for a year in the City Hospital. Towards the end of my surgical training, I worked in Lurgan under the surgeon Jack Balmer. He was a great help to me because he would set me questions for my forthcoming exams and correct the answers.

'During this time, I was also studying to become a Fellow of the Royal College of Surgeons [FRCS], which is essential if you want to become a consultant surgeon. I managed to pass the first part of the FRCS in Dublin, after my usual need to persevere after struggling with the course. After a period of intense study and a fair amount of stress, I succeeded in passing my final FRCS exam which was held in Edinburgh in 1962. It was a great relief because after years of living with very little money and struggling to buy just the basics, I knew I would now be able to pay off some of the debts I had accrued while studying.'

'That must have been an amazing feeling. I can remember you telling me how good it felt to go and see the bank manager after you got your first consultant job and being able to pay off all of your debts in one go. I would imagine you went from persona non grata to a valued customer overnight.'

'Yes, it was a great feeling all right. I have always understood the value of money, because when you don't have it, life can sometimes be a real struggle. I felt I had achieved something significant and, more importantly, as I always say to you, I had persevered and that was what mattered.'

Besides the academia, Dad continued to play rugby at university. When he went to Queen's, there were plenty of rugby players who had already established themselves. Being a fresher, Dad had to prove himself and was initially chosen to play for a junior team. I was curious how he found out he'd been chosen to play his first game of rugby at university.

'I can still recall it vividly. I was doing a chemistry practical on a Friday afternoon and someone came in and gave me a little note which said: "You have been chosen to play for the First XV tomorrow against Bective Rangers, be at the railway station to catch the early morning train to Dublin."

'I wondered why I had been chosen and later found out that the out-half, Derek Monteith, had broken his leg. I used to say the cynic might remark that it was a lucky break for me! By the time Derek's leg had healed, Ernie Strathdee and I had established ourselves as half-backs and Derek moved to centre, a position that also suited him and the one in which he played when he captained Ireland in 1947.

'My rugby career seemed to take off from there really. I was chosen to play for Ulster – I remember a wonderful game against a Kiwi Army side at Ravenhill in November 1945, where Ulster were defeated by the narrowest of margins, 10–9. It was a thrilling match and we came very close to beating them. Jack Finlay scored a try, which was worth three points, and they also scored a drop goal, worth four points at the time, and a penalty goal, which was also worth three points. We managed a try and two penalties.

'That Kiwi side toured Britain and Ireland at the end of the war and helped to revive the interest in rugby. There was incredible talent and some remarkable players on that New Zealand side, including Bob Scott and Freddy Alan as well as Charlie Sexton, their captain.

'During the war years, no official internationals were played between the home countries and France, but every December from about 1941, an Irish XV played the British Army at Ravenhill. I was chosen to play in this game in 1945 when I was nineteen, along with another young nineteen-year-old, Karl Mullen, who later captained Ireland as well as the Lions for the 1950 tour to New Zealand and Australia. Although we were very young, it wasn't unusual

The Irish XV that played the British Army XV on 15 December 1945 – I'm sitting on the ground on the left. This was my debut for Ireland, and another debutant, Karl Mullen, is seated behind me, second from the right.

for schoolboys to receive international caps in those days, as the Hewitt brothers had done, but for a forward to be chosen at the age of nineteen was something special, so it was a great achievement for Karl.

'I remember that game vividly because it was my first big game – and also because I scored a try. My opposite number was a famous rugby league player called Gus Risman, whose son Beverly later played rugby (union) for England.

'In 1946, unofficial internationals started between the four home countries and France, but no international caps were awarded. It was during one of these matches – I can't remember exactly which match it was, but I think it may have been against England – that I received the only severe injury I ever had during my rugby career. I was going to pick up the ball, and I collided with one of my own players, injuring my left ankle.

'I was moved out to the left wing for the remainder of the game, where I had very little to do. In those days, injured players often went to see the trainer at Glentoran Football Club, who was called Billie Ritchie, and he advised them how best to treat the injury. However, the orthopaedic surgeon Mr Withers from the Royal Victoria happened to be in Dublin at the match and I received a message that he wished to see me after the game.

'My father drove me to the hospital where Mr Withers asked me if I'd had an x-ray taken, to which I sheepishly replied that I hadn't. He immediately insisted I get one. When the x-ray came back, no fracture showed up, but as Mr Withers was an expert on injuries of the lateral ligament of the ankle, he took another x-ray of the ankle in acute inversion. After studying this x-ray, he told me that the ligament was completely ruptured. The timing was not good, as there were away games against Wales and Scotland coming up and I'd hoped to play in them.

When Mr Withers informed me that he was going to put my ankle in a short leg plaster for a month, my face dropped. He advised me to discuss it with my father but because my father had a great respect for Mr Withers, he told me that I was to do exactly as I was told. The plaster went on and I went back to the fracture clinic a month later, hoping to have it taken off so I could play in the final game of the season, but when Mr Withers looked at the ankle, he said to the orthopaedic sister, "Strengthen that plaster and bring him back in a month's time."

'That put an end to all rugby for that season. In spite of my disappointment at missing those matches – even though no caps were awarded because they were unofficial internationals – I look back with enormous gratitude for what Mr Withers did for me, as my ankle never troubled me again during my career. Had Mr Withers not insisted on proper healing time for that ankle ligament, I could have ended up with an unstable ankle, because the lateral ligament is very important in stabilising the ankle joint. I now understand the importance of giving time to ligaments and bones to heal properly and I often wonder if professional rugby players today are returning to play too soon after an injury.

'I returned to rugby in time for the 1947 season. I would always stay in bed the morning of an international match and order a late breakfast to the room. I always took things very easy on the day of a match. If the game was in Dublin, we travelled down on the Friday morning and we were put up in the Shelbourne Hotel. We would have a quick run out on the Friday afternoon where you met your scrum-half and worked out signals. We would travel to the game by coach as a team. I always felt a bit keyed up but generally OK before a game. I do remember on one occasion, lying in bed on the morning before a

The Irish XV that beat England 22-0 at Lansdowne Road in 1947.

TELEGRAPHIC ADDRESS,
"FOOTBALL, DUBLIN."
TELEPHONE Nº 21984.

IRISH RUGBY FOOTBALL UNION,

14, WESTMORELAND STREET,

DUBLIN.

Date 10th February, 1947

DEAR SI..

I have pleasure in advising that you have been selected to play for :—

Ireland v. Scotland.

At Murrayfield, Edinburgh.

On Saturday 22nd February, 1947

and shall be glad to receive your **early** acceptance.

The team will travel in reserved accommodation
via .... by .... train
leaving .... Station.

You are requested to be present at .... to receive Travelling Ticket.

Headquarters North British Hotel Edinburgh
where programme of final arrangements will be issued.

Your jersey will be supplied, and must be returned immediately at the conclusion of the game.

The Irish Union provide transportation and pay Hotel Expenses, including gratuities to servants, but do not hold themselves responsible for personal tips, telegrams, 'phone calls, etc., etc., given by Members of the Team. Should you, however, incur any other legitimate expenses, please furnish on attached Form to Hon. Treasurer.

Yours truly,
RUPERT W. JEFFARES, *Secretary.*

Please bring one pair clean white knicks.
There will be a charge of 30/- on any
player not returning his jersey after
the Match. Apply to Mr. J. E. Hamilton
for all travelling arrangements. Players
to supply own towel and soap

The official notice from the IRFU to say I'd been selected to play against Scotland in February 1947.

big game and wondering what would happen if I really messed up, but most of the time I took it as it came and managed to use my adrenaline to help with my game.

'In 1947, the official internationals started and I was selected to play in all four of them that year – in those days, Ireland only played against England, Scotland Wales and France. France had been allowed back into the competition the previous year, after an absence of sixteen years that had been caused by issues of administration and professionalism. From what I understand, the French had been suspended from the competition in 1931 because of what was seen as an abuse of the rules of the amateur game by the French Rugby Federation.

'On 8 February 1947, Ireland defeated England at Lansdowne Road by the biggest margin they had ever suffered at the hands of Ireland, 22–0. The team was captained by the great Con Murphy from Lansdowne Rugby Club, who was full-back. We then travelled to Scotland and defeated them 3–0 at Murrayfield. I always enjoyed staying at the North British Hotel as we dined in a room with a magnificent view over Princes Street. We lost to France (12–8) and Wales (6–0), with Wales defeating us to win the Triple Crown. We played Wales in Swansea, which was a ground at which we were told to be careful, because the touchline ran at an angle. It was disappointing having beaten England so comprehensively that we didn't manage to do better against France and Wales, but despite

Playing for Ulster against a British Army side, 1952.

our disappointment I thoroughly enjoyed my first Five Nations Tournament.

'From 1946 to my retirement, I also played many matches for Ulster – mainly against Leinster, Munster and Connaught, in what was known as the Inter-Provincial Championship. I always enjoyed those matches enormously, especially given my love for travel, getting to go to Dublin, Cork, Limerick and Galway. As there were so many inter-provincial matches over the years, I can no longer remember all the results, but I know Ulster won the Inter-Provincial Championship in 1946 and then Leinster won it for two years consecutively in 1947 and 1948.

'I also played for Ulster against two English county sides. We played Lancashire in October 1948 and won 8–0 and my brother Eric partnered me in that game at half-back in place of Ernie Strathdee – I think the selectors wanted to see how Eric would play, as he had played well against a British Army side in the previous season. It was a great pleasure to play alongside him. Lancashire beat us the following year by a point, 15–14. Their forwards were very strong and it was a tough match. We also played Yorkshire in October 1949 and won 29–14. These games stopped later in the 1950s because the rugby schedule became too busy.

'In the 1940s and early 1950s, there was also a trial match every year between the Combined Universities of Ireland and a team called the Rest of Ireland. I played in many of these games for Queen's University and I thoroughly enjoyed them. Most of the teams were from UCD or other universities from the South, but Ernie Strathdee, Harry Millar and myself represented Queen's in many of those games.

'The other games in which I played for Ireland or Ulster would have been against touring sides, such as the game I previously mentioned in November 1945 when Ulster played really well against a touring New Zealand side, losing to them by only a point.

'So aside from playing for Ireland, there were plenty of games to be played for Ulster. I loved my time playing for Ulster as well as Ireland. I also played many games for Queen's while up at university, so most Saturdays you would probably find me on a rugby pitch somewhere! Despite all the rugby, I still managed to find enough time to study and get my qualifications, and I would say that my time at Queen's University was one of the happiest times of my life.'

CHAPTER FOUR

THE GRAND SLAM YEAR

'La nature fait le mérite et la fortune le met en oeuvre.'
François de La Rochefoucauld

In February 2013, as the Six Nations tournament kicked off, rugby fever gripped Ireland again and I felt the usual excitement and anticipation building up. I visited Dad the day before one of Ireland's matches, which seemed like an opportune time to ask him about the year he won the Grand Slam. I arrived in Bryansford on a Saturday morning, made us a coffee and my only request to Dad was that he told me everything in as much detail as he could remember about that 1948 season.

❁

'1948 was a great year for Irish rugby, but the significance of our Grand Slam-winning side was not obvious at the time. Our stature grew over the decades when no other team repeated our success. It took sixty-one years for Ireland to win another Grand Slam, although we did come close in 1951.

'The first Irish game in 1948 was against France in Paris, played on 1 January, which was a Thursday. This was purely coincidental, we didn't usually play games on New Year's Day but it just fell that way. Travel in those days was a very different affair. There was no hopping on and off a plane journey lasting an hour or so. The players from the North travelled to Dublin, where we met the rest of the Irish players. Then we all took a boat from Dublin to Holyhead and then a train from Holyhead to London, changing at Crewe. We stayed in London for the night and the next day travelled by train from London to Dover, crossing the channel by ferry to Calais and then taking the train from Calais to Paris. So we arrived in Paris two days before the game, after two days of travelling.

'The international side only got together the day before the match – we didn't meet beforehand for training or talks about tactics – we only had a run-out to exercise our legs for about half an hour in the stadium. In Paris, it was at the Stade de Colombes, and we passed the ball amongst the three-quarters and worked out signals with the scrum-half. After this, we returned to the hotel

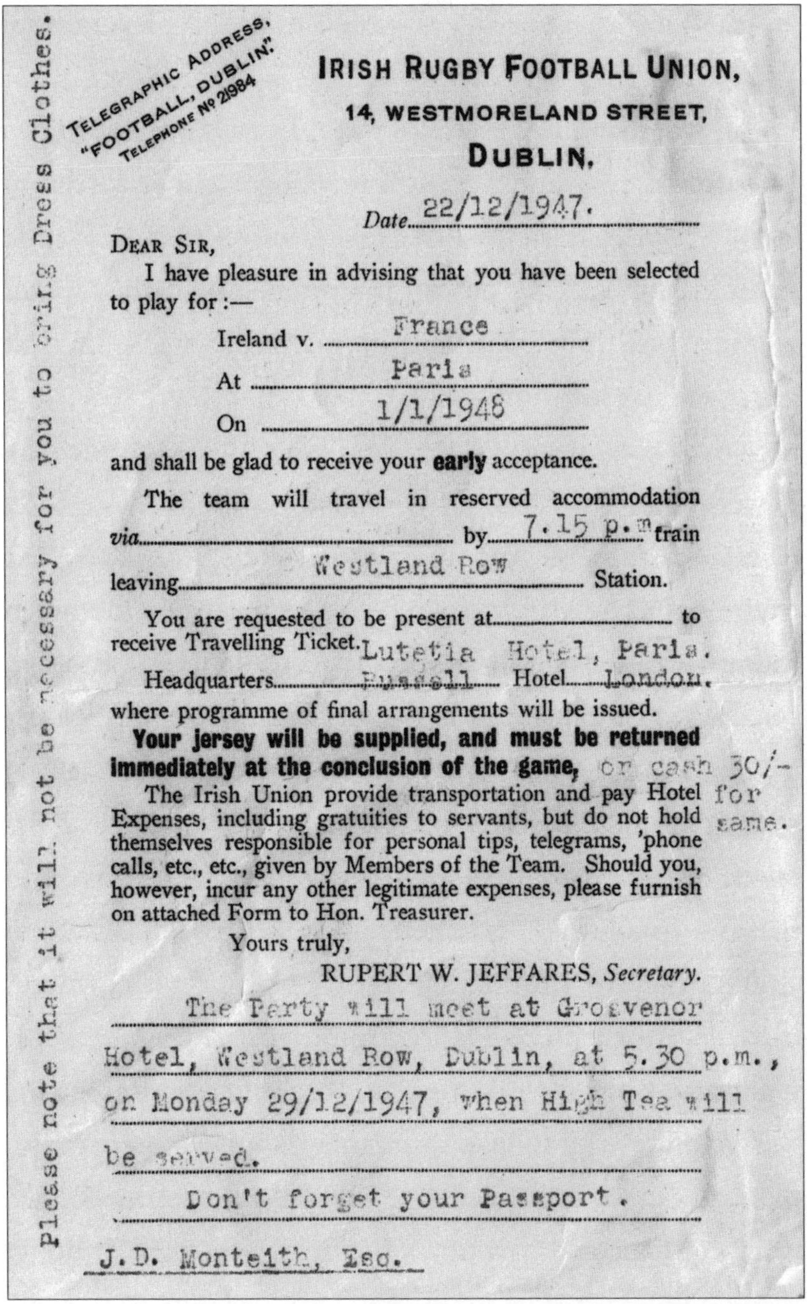

TELEGRAPHIC ADDRESS,
"FOOTBALL, DUBLIN."
TELEPHONE Nº 21984

IRISH RUGBY FOOTBALL UNION,
14, WESTMORELAND STREET,
DUBLIN.

Date 22/12/1947.

DEAR SIR,

I have pleasure in advising that you have been selected to play for :—

Ireland v. France

At Paris

On 1/1/1948

and shall be glad to receive your **early** acceptance.

The team will travel in reserved accommodation *via* .... by 7.15 p.m. train leaving Westland Row Station.

You are requested to be present at .... to receive Travelling Ticket. Lutetia Hotel, Paris.

Headquarters Russell Hotel London.

where programme of final arrangements will be issued.

Your jersey will be supplied, and must be returned immediately at the conclusion of the game, or cash 30/- for same.

The Irish Union provide transportation and pay Hotel Expenses, including gratuities to servants, but do not hold themselves responsible for personal tips, telegrams, 'phone calls, etc., etc., given by Members of the Team. Should you, however, incur any other legitimate expenses, please furnish on attached Form to Hon. Treasurer.

Yours truly,

RUPERT W. JEFFARES, *Secretary.*

The Party will meet at Grosvenor Hotel, Westland Row, Dublin, at 5.30 p.m., on Monday 29/12/1947, when High Tea will be served.

Don't forget your Passport.

J.D. Monteith, Esq.

Please note that it will not be necessary for you to bring Dress Clothes.

The official notice from the IRFU to say I'd been selected to play against France on New Year's Day, 1948.

and had a team meeting at which only the players were present.

'In the amateur days, there was no coach or manager to give instructions and the team meeting was a very relaxed affair – to be honest, we didn't take it very seriously. We felt you did your talking out on the pitch. The team captain would sit in front of us and he might ask, "Has anyone got any ideas for tomorrow?"

'With the professional era, everything about the players is carefully monitored and controlled – from their nutrition, and every other aspect of their health, to their training and down time. This is all accepted as the norm today because players have become a valuable commodity, but I watch the professional game with huge relief that I am not a part of it. It was so very different in my day. In 1948, the night before the French game, the team were taken to the Folies Bergère – it was New Year's Eve, and it was a totally new experience for a group of Irishmen. Even though we thoroughly enjoyed the spectacle, we still managed to get to bed before midnight. I think however it gives new meaning to the idea of relaxing before a game!

'Well, the – by today's standards – unusual preparation paid off, as we unexpectedly defeated France [13–6]. We were not expected to win, as they had beaten us at home the previous year. The stadium in Paris was very impressive and we had to come through a long tunnel and out on to the pitch, which not every stadium had in those days. If

I remember correctly, it was a wet day and that may have helped us a bit.

'We played Scotland next on 28 February at Lansdowne Road and we won that game 6–0, I scored one of the tries in that game and Barney Mullen scored the other, though neither was converted. Of course, it is always that bit special playing in front of your home crowd. I played against Scotland about ten times in my career and I was never on a losing side.

'Our next game was against England in Twickenham where we had a narrow victory by one point. I scored a try in that game from a scrum near the English twenty-five, but I also made a mistake – I caught the ball near their twenty-five and decided to open up play, so I ran across the field to line up with my own three-quarters. However, I threw out a pass that was intercepted by Dickie Guest, the England wing three-quarters, who did not stop until he had put the ball underneath our posts. This took the score from 11–5 in our favour to 11–10. I did not enjoy the final ten to fifteen minutes of the game, to put it mildly. I had to sweat it out until the final whistle, but we managed to hold on and win despite my error. I can tell you it was quite a relief to hear the final whistle.

'Our final game to win the Grand Slam was against Wales and was played at Ravenhill on 13 March 1948. Ireland had not won the Grand Slam since 1899, when that team had also won the Triple Crown. It had been a

Jack Daly scoring the try that won the Grand Slam, 1948.

long ten weeks since our first match in Paris, and Wales were a very hard side to play against – their marking was so good it was difficult to make a break in the three-quarter line. We managed to strike the first blow with a try scored by Barney Mullen on the left wing, but before half-time Wales replied with a score by Bleddyn Williams. In the second half, we broke Welsh hearts early with a try by Jack Daly, our front-row forward, after he picked up a forward dribble. When Daly was walking back to the halfway line after having scored the try, he said, "If Wales don't score again, I'll be canonised!"

'There was great rejoicing when the final whistle went and we'd won – I remember the crowd rushing onto the field and carrying off some of the players. We could hardly get off the pitch for all the people.

'Jack Daly had the shirt torn from his back and it was reported that pieces of it were being sold many months later to enthusiastic collectors. We never imagined for one second that it would be sixty-one years before Ireland would win another Grand Slam.

'Winning that Grand Slam has meant we have dined out on many occasions and it has opened many doors for us in the way of invitations and publicity. Since then, Ireland has won several Triple Crowns, but, although we came close, we never managed to clinch another Grand Slam during my playing career.

'It is amazing how much times have changed. I read an article in *The Irish Times* comparing the cost of tickets in 1948 and 2009. In 1948, a ticket for the game cost the equivalent of sixty-four cent and a match programme cost three shillings, which would be about 1.5 cent!

'For that first French match on News Year's Day, Ernie Strathdee captained the Irish side but, unusually for the winning captain, he was dropped for the next two games and Hugh De Lacy took his place against Scotland and England. Then Ernie Strathdee was brought back to play against Wales. He was considered to be bigger and stronger than Hugh De Lacy and it was felt that he could face up to the Welsh forwards better than Hugh. I enjoyed playing with Hugh, and I scored a try every time we played together. I felt sorry for him when he lost his place for the final match against Wales.

'After Ernie Strathdee was dropped, my friend Karl Mullen, who was the hooker, captained the Irish side for

IRISH RUGBY FOOTBALL UNION

SCOTLAND v IRELAND

At EDINBURGH

SATURDAY, 26th FEBRUARY, 1949

Official Itinerary

THURSDAY, 24th FEBRUARY

5.00p.m.   Report at Amiens Street Station, Dublin, to collect Travel Tickets.

5.30 p.m.   Leave by "Enterprise" train for Belfast. Dine en route.

7.45 p.m.   Due Belfast. Bus awaiting at Station for transfer to Burns Laird Steamer, Donegall Quay, Belfast.

8.30 p.m.   Leave for Glasgow. Each passenger will be provided with through ticket via Glasgow to Edinburgh, together with Sleeping Berth card giving Cabin No. on board, and similar for return journey by Larne-Stranraer. PASSPORTS or Travel Permits must be ready for inspection of Immigration Officials at time of embarkation.

FRIDAY, 25th FEBRUARY

7.00 a.m.   Approximate time of arrival at Glasgow.

8.00 a.m.   Breakfast on board (present voucher supplied to dining room steward).

9.00 a.m.   Buses in attendance for transfer to Queen Street Station, Glasgow.

9.45 a.m.   At Queen Street.

10.00 a.m.   Queen Street Station train leaves for Edinburgh.

11.11 a.m.   Due arrive Waverley Station, Edinburgh. Proceed to Irish XV Headquarters, North British Hotel, adjacent to station.

12.45 p.m.   Lunch. Private room reserved for meals (Official Party only).

3.00 p.m.   Leave by bus for training (team should have their complete club outfit).

6.30 p.m.   Dinner in Official Private Room. Team will be advised of any entertainment.

SATURDAY, 26th FEBRUARY

10.30 a.m. / 12.30 p.m.   Lunch in Official Private Room.

1.45 p.m.   Bus from Hotel to Murrayfield.

3.00 p.m.   Kick-off.

5.00 p.m.   Bus returns from Murrayfield to N.B. Hotel.

6.45–7 p.m.   Complimentary Dinner to Irish XV. Details as per Scottish Invitation Card. Evening Dress. Dinner Jackets.

The itinerary for the first part of the trip to Murrayfield for the game against Scotland, 1949.

the next three or four years. Karl and I enjoyed a lifelong friendship until his death in 2009.

'The victories in 1948 and 1949 brought me much more to the attention of the public. I didn't mind being recognised and found it a very pleasant experience to be part of a winning team. I didn't mind the loss of privacy, not that there was much loss of privacy. The hype that has come in with the professional era simply didn't exist in my day. I imagine if any of us had even had thoughts above our station, we would have been brought back down to earth by our team very quickly, not to mention friends and family. It was also frowned upon by the rugby authorities for a player to give interviews or write articles for the papers about their rugby career whilst they were still playing. My father, with his emphasis on the importance of my medical career, always kept my feet firmly planted on the ground. It wasn't like the game today where you are subjected to so much media scrutiny – we were largely left in peace.

'In 1949, Ireland secured a Triple Crown, losing only to France. We were delighted by this, as it was this that was seen as a great achievement. The Triple Crown was talked about a lot more in those days than the Grand Slam, which I know may seem a bit strange, but it had a great history behind it and it was seen as a real achievement to beat England, Scotland and Wales. As the great rugby journalist Edmund Van Esbeck noted on the sixtieth anniversary of the 1948 win: "In those days there was no talk about a Grand Slam. Indeed, not one contemporary report of the [Wales] match mentioned it. The Triple Crown was the Holy Grail and Ireland had reached the Promised Land."

'We secured our second Triple Crown in March 1949 at St Helen's Park in Swansea in Wales, beating the Welsh 5–0. It was our first win in Wales for seventeen years, so we were thrilled altogether. If I remember rightly, I kicked the ball high to the right after a scrum inside the Welsh twenty-five and Jim McCarthy leapt up like a gazelle and scored a try that George Norton converted, and that was our win.

Jim McCarthy scores the try against Wales that wins the Triple Crown and the Championship, 1949.

'After that Wales game, both teams attended a dinner along with both presidents of the respective rugby unions and other officials. Compared to the celebrations that you see today after sports games, we were much more relaxed about it all.

'In 1950, Wales won the Triple Crown but, in 1951, we came very close again to another championship win. We beat France [9–8] in Dublin. We then went on to beat England [3–0] in another home game, which also happened to fall on my twenty-fifth birthday, so it was a double celebration, and following that we beat Scotland in Edinburgh [6–5], but we drew against Wales in Cardiff, 3–3.

'In that match against Wales, I scored a try as a result of some inter-passing amongst the backs, before I received the ball and touched down. A try in those days was worth three points, and Wales kicked a penalty, which was also three points. We had a few more penalty opportunities which we missed as we were without George Norton, our regular place-kicker. So although we had one of our best years, we won neither a Triple Crown nor a Grand Slam, because draws didn't count.

'1951 was the year Cliff Morgan was first chosen to play for Wales. Cliff was a brilliant rugby player who, when he toured with the Lions to South Africa in 1955, was considered the best out-half who had ever played in South Africa. Cliff and I became great friends – and I was very saddened by his recent death. Cliff was an immensely

Meeting up with the rest of the team before the match against England, 1951.

Eating lemons at half-time in the match against England at Lansdowne Road, 1951.

Signing autographs at the end of the match against England at Lansdowne Road, 1951.

talented rugby player and had a great rugby brain. He was a great talker and superb after-dinner speaker – which you could guess given his very successful career in broadcasting. It was very sad that cancer caused the need to have his larynx removed, so there was no more of the wonderful oratory that had delighted so many people. I will miss his friendship, his wonderful talks and his great sense of humour. Cecil Pedlow, Mary Peters and I went over to the Isle of Wight for his eightieth birthday and Cliff, with wonderful courage and keeping his finger in the opening of his tracheostomy, thanked us all for coming to help him celebrate. I also remember on my eightieth birthday, Cliff sent me a case of fabulous wines. I wrote to him and said in the letter: "You are definitely raising my standard of wine drinking with such great vintages."

'Post-match dinners in the 1940s and 1950s were very different to those of today. Many rugby players in those days were teetotal and I recall at the wonderful French banquet after a game in Paris, there were six glasses in front of each place with a different vintage for every course. When the wine waiter came around to pour the wine for each course, I would put my hand over the glass and say, "Non, merci, avez-vous un jus de fruits?" I am sure the waiter must have been thinking, *Look at this nutcase passing up on all these incredible vintages, the likes of which he may never have the opportunity to drink again!*

I have to agree with him now and I am making up for it as best I can!

'We have dined out on winning the Grand Slam on many occasions since then and we did have a reunion of the 1948 side in 2008 – there were seven of us and it was great to meet up with old friends from that era. We certainly enjoyed the excellent wine provided on that occasion.

'There's a great story that sums up how much sport can give you and how many sportsmen profit from their achievements. After winning his gold medal in 1956, Ronnie Delaney received huge press attention and this went on for a long time, as it is not often Ireland can boast having an Olympic gold-medal winner. Ronnie told me that he had been in Dublin city centre one day and a man came up to him and in a strong Dublin brogue said, "Are you Ronnie Delaney?" Ronnie said he was, to which the man replied, "You know, Mr Delaney, you've got an awful lot of mileage out of running that one mile!"'

CHAPTER FIVE

BECOMING
A LION

'The most unforgettable character I have ever met.'
Winston McCarthy, New Zealand commentator
and journalist, speaking about Dad

Before I started to talk to Dad about the 1950 Lions tour, we decided that there was no need for him to talk about every match that took place – so much more happened than just rugby and there have already been plenty of books written about the games, giving a blow-by-blow account of every match on the tour. Dad is as interested in talking about some of the other aspects of the tour as much as the rugby. The first thing I wanted to ask about was how he found out he had been selected.

❁

'In 1949, the Rugby Union asked me if I'd be able to go on the tour to Australia and New Zealand if I was selected. Naturally, I thought this was a great honour and without saying anything to anyone else in the family, I said I would. In those days, the Rugby Union often didn't inform families that their sons had been selected; the team list just appeared in the papers.

'My father found out about my involvement with the Lions when he was sitting in his study reading the *Belfast Telegraph* and saw the article listing the players who had been chosen to go on the six-month tour. I had to laugh at his reaction. It wasn't a case of: "My son has been chosen to play for the Lions, what an honour!" Instead, I was told by my siblings that he was none too pleased to have read it in the paper as a done deal and felt that my studying to become a doctor was far more important than going on the tour, which he thought could adversely affect my studies. Fortunately, I wasn't at home at the time, but my brother Eric had to listen to the tirade of comments as my irate father asked him rather rhetorically, "Does that brother of yours ever intend to qualify in medicine?"

'When I did return home later, my father had calmed down somewhat, but I had quite a job persuading him that I could manage the tour without it affecting my studies and I could make up any time I lost.

'I told him that three months of the tour were during the university holidays, and that I could make up the other three months the following year. The important thing was to pass the medical exams at the end of fourth year, which I had to do before the tour started. With this decided, my father agreed that I could go – though he was still a little reluctant. It sounds as if my father was very strict but he just wanted to make me realise the importance of my career. I knew he was quietly pleased about my selection!'

I am sure my grandfather must have been proud of Dad, but he knew Dad would have to earn a living after his rugby career was over and understandably that was his primary concern.

The 1950s Lions squad had thirteen Welshmen, nine Irishmen, five Scotsmen and three Englishmen. Karl Mullen, from Ireland, was made captain at the age of twenty-three. The reason so many Welshmen were selected was because Wales had won the Triple Crown in 1950 – which just goes to show that some things don't change, given that there were so many Welshman on the 2013 tour for the same reason.

Sadly, those Triple Crown celebrations of 1950 were tempered because the plane taking Welsh supporters back to Wales crashed and eighty people were killed. The aircraft, an Avro Tudor V, had been privately hired to fly rugby supporters to and from the international game at Ravenhill and the crash, which was caused by a stall, happened as the plane tried to land at Llandow. The Llandow Air Disaster was a terrible tragedy and the dead were remembered on 25 March when Wales played France at Cardiff Arms Park in the final game of the 1950 Championship. The crowd stood in silence while five buglers sounded the 'Last Post' in tribute to those who had died.

The manager on the Lions tour was Ginger Osborne, who was a captain in the Royal Navy and a dentist. A sign of how differently things were done back then is that only one reporter travelled with the team – Dai Gent from *The Sunday Times*. Dad had a great respect for Dai, who had been a headmaster and had played scrum-half for England in the early 1900s.

'Dai was a family man and found the tour somewhat exhausting – he was sixty-seven at the time. Everywhere he went, he was questioned by New Zealanders about the try that the All Blacks, under the captaincy of Dave Gallaher, were "supposed" to have scored against Wales in 1905 – the try was disallowed and it was the only game that the All Blacks lost on their tour. I guess people thought Dai may have been at the game as he was playing around the same time and they wanted his opinion on it.

Dai, who was a quiet, contemplative man, found the tour difficult, as there were only two games played each week and there was a lot of time to fill in between. He went home after about two months, leaving no official reporter with the tour. There were some reports in the local papers, which were then copied by the British and Irish papers.

Compared with the Lions tours of today, where dozens of sports journalists and photographers travel with the team, as well as the matches being televised all over the world, it was a very quiet tour.'

'What did it feel like, heading off at the young age of twenty-four to travel such a long distance?'

'Well, I just remember feeling excited, with perhaps a few nerves, but the overriding feeling was one of great anticipation for the adventure that lay ahead – I had always yearned to travel and experience new countries and cultures. I was also aware that I wanted to do myself proud in the matches and my main hope was to play in all four test matches in New Zealand and the two in Australia.

'I was one of those players who didn't think about what I was doing on the rugby field. In fact, the more I thought about it, the worse I played. I remember once at North Rugby Club consciously thinking that I was going to go out there and really impress everyone. It was the worst I have ever played and, after the game, I said to myself, "Don't ever do that again. You have just got to wait for your opportunities. Just go out there and do what you do. Don't think about it." I guess you could say I played on instinct.

'There were thirty selected Lions and management and we set off from Euston Station at about 10.30 a.m. on Saturday, 1 April 1950. We were given our Lions blazers and a talk by the Colonial Secretary of the time, telling us that

SS Ceramic.

we had to behave well at all times, as we were representing Britain and Ireland. We then took the train from London to Liverpool and boarded the ship, named the SS *Ceramic*, which was part of the Shaw-Savill Shipping Line. It was a small ship that had been used in the past to carry sheep and lambs from New Zealand to the UK.

'It took four weeks to sail to New Zealand, crossing the Atlantic, going through the Panama Canal and then out into the Pacific Ocean. There was plenty of time for reading, and to keep fit we would run around the top deck of the ship. Although I had brought my books to study, I have to say I didn't do much with them, but instead I picked the brain of Karl Mullen who was studying gynaecology and midwifery.

'After a few days, during which some of the players suffered with seasickness, life on board settled down to something of a routine. We did a bit of physical training each day at about 11.30 a.m. – some exercises and perhaps a run around the deck. After lunch, we would get together and discuss rugby and the various tactics that could be used against the All Blacks. I seldom read any books about the game, and all this talk about rugby and its moves was a real eye-opener for me. The height of our team talks came courtesy of the medical staff, and included simple advice such as the importance of everyone getting a good night's sleep and the importance of not overindulging whilst we were on board ship by eating or drinking too much.

'I shared a cabin with Bill McKay and Jim McCarthy, and, as I was the youngest, I had to take the upper bunk! Bill was a wing-forward from Queen's who had fought in the war and been with the Gurkhas in the Burmese jungle. He was a man who kept himself very fit and was a very good mile runner – he ran Roger Bannister a close second in a race in the 1940s.

'Jim and I have been lifelong friends and are still in touch. When I came back from Zambia, I, along with my sister Betty, frequently went down to stay with Jim and his wife Pat at their home in County Clare. On one occasion, when I was home on leave and was staying in Dublin after a dinner, Jim invited me to play golf the following morning. I did not expect to see him quite so early and was rather surprised to get a knock on the door at about 6.30 for our round of golf. We were out on Portmarnock golf course by 7 a.m. and Jim was delighted to be able to enjoy the beauty and peace of the course, as there wasn't

Travelling on SS Ceramic – we spent alot of time relaxing but managed to do some training too.

another soul around at that hour. I was not playing well and I remarked that I would have to practise a bit more in Zambia, to which Jim drily replied, "You'll only be practising your faults."

'Jim was a good golfer and at one time played off a handicap of one or two, whereas my best ever handicap out in Zambia was eleven. I always enjoyed the game of golf, but it was certainly not a game that came easily to me, and during the times when I played badly, I had to keep reminding myself it was good exercise and was supposed to be relaxing!

'Shortly after we left Liverpool on the Lions tour, at about ten o'clock in the evening, someone remarked that they were a bit hungry and could do with something to eat just to finish off the evening. Tom Clifford, a wonderful character from Munster, invited us to his cabin where he pulled out a huge trunk and opened it. It was filled with all sorts of goodies, such as baked cakes, pies and other delicacies, which his mother, Mrs Clifford, had obviously been baking for a long time beforehand. In the way that many Irish mothers do, she had become used to feeding a large growing lad and worried that Tom may not get enough to eat whilst he was away, which she felt certainly wouldn't do. And Tom did have quite the appetite. On one evening, the team decided to have an eating competition, by attempting to eat their way through the whole menu on board. Tom won hands down by going through each of the nineteen options and Bill McKay came in second finishing off thirteen. Tom is always fondly remembered for his generosity in sharing his trunk load of snacks with the team. We spent many evenings tucking into these goodies in Tom's cabin before going to bed. Following some discussion amongst the team, we decided to write Mrs Clifford a thank you note for all the lovely food we had enjoyed. Tom was a great character and the heart and soul of any party.

'After dinner on occasion, the team amused themselves with each team member being called on to do a party piece. Tom Clifford always used to sing 'O'Reilly's Daughter' and I can still remember it:

As I was walking down the street
Who should I see but the one-eyed Reilly
With two pistols in his hand looking for the man that
  married his daughter.
'Yiddeee aye oh ... yideeee aye ay.'

'So, what was your party piece, Dad?'

'Ah, sure, you know I wasn't a great singer, but I managed to get away with a song which I had first heard in Galway by Charlie St George called 'My Uncle Dan McCann', which I could pass off by almost talking rather than singing. Many an Irish person will be familiar with the song and Noel [Henderson] and I often used to do this one at parties together.

'One of the verses was:

I am lately landed over here to look for me Uncle Dan,
*   he left the County Galway about the year of 61,*
If any old neighbour living here has seen or heard of
*   him, you'll oblige me if you'll help me find me Uncle*
*   Dan McCann.*
My uncle was a mighty man in Erin's land they say; he
*   swam the river Liffey twice a day*
He ran all round the Phoenix Park, he could dance and
*   sing just like a lark*
He wasn't afraid to go home in the dark, me Uncle Dan
*   McCann!*

'There were only eighty passengers on the ship and unfortunately, or perhaps fortunately, for the rugby team, there was only one eligible young lady on board who was the tender age of fifteen.

People often ask me why on earth we went by ship, as it would have been possible to fly to New Zealand, but apparently it was too expensive to insure the lives of so many players, so it was more economical to travel by ship.

'The boat sailed into the Atlantic and our first stop was Curaçao in the West Indies, where we were able to disembark and soak up this highly unique and unusual culture. A lot of the players, including myself, had never been outside Europe, so it was a fascinating experience. From

Sailing through the Panama Canal.

Curaçao, we sailed to the Panama Canal and stopped at Panama City where we were allowed a short break off the ship. That evening a crowd of us all went to a nightclub that was run by a man called Murphy – the humour of this was not lost on us and we told him that his forbearers were probably Irish, although he was clearly of West Indian extraction!

'From Panama City, we sailed into the Pacific Ocean and didn't stop for two weeks until we reached Wellington, approximately one month after leaving Liverpool. We had hoped to stop at Pitcairn Island where the descendants of the sailors who mutinied on the *Bounty* in 1789 lived, but, unfortunately, the ship's captain told us that as we would arrive at Pitcairn Island before midnight, he couldn't wait until the following morning for the islanders to arrive – they often met ships to sell their produce.

'We were on board ship for thirty-one days and we provided our own entertainment – a lot of players were only too happy to invent games and competitions. During the trip, I also received a telegram from my brother Eric, with the news that his wife Jacqueline had given birth to a beautiful son, who was named Stewart. My first nephew – I was delighted. A second son was born to them a few years later, who was christened Eric, after his father. Being away for family events like that did make you miss home a little, but for the most part we were too busy enjoying ourselves to give much thought to anything else!

'We finally arrived in Wellington Harbour on Tuesday, 2 May 1950. There are some good pictures of us coming down the gangway of the ship. I had read a fair bit about New Zealand and its people, and I couldn't wait to see what the country was like and also to start playing some rugby.

'After receptions by the New Zealand Rugby Union in Wellington and a dance for the players, we crossed from

Arriving in Wellington.

Getting ready to leave the Ceramic *after we arrived in Wellington (l–r):
Jim McCarthy, Noel, me and Ranald Macdonald.*

Wellington to Nelson in the north of the North Island. There was at that time, I recall, a dolphin called Jack, that met the ship leaving Wellington, guided it all the way into Nelson and met it when it was leaving Nelson and guided it all the way back to Wellington. It was a glorious sight to watch him swimming in front of the ship. Perhaps he sensed there were some new visitors on board.

'I remember one beautiful morning walking with Noel [Henderson] and seeing a kingfisher flying and swooping over the river as we took in the view over a beautiful old bridge into a splendid river below. The scenery in New Zealand really was magnificent, we were all so impressed by the country and it added a great deal of pleasure to the tour.'

'So, what else did you do in Wellington when you weren't playing rugby?'

'There was plenty of time for socialising. When Noel and I were in Wellington, we were talking to a lady at one of the many functions we attended, who, when we told her we were headed for Nelson, said, "Oh, I have two lovely nieces in Nelson, you must look them up when you are there."

'It didn't take Noel twice to be asked! He willingly took the details of the two sisters and assured their aunt that he would indeed look them up when we arrived. Not being one to waste an opportunity, we had barely set foot in Nelson when Noel told me we were going to visit the two sisters that evening.

'Upon arriving at the door and explaining that we had met his sister-in-law in Wellington, the girls' father informed us that, unfortunately, the two girls were out, but that he would be delighted for us to come in and wait, as he expected them back very shortly. We found out that this man had fought in the First World War and been involved in some of the most brutal battles and had consequently been invalided out.

'Shortly afterwards the two girls arrived and Noel and I were introduced to Jean and Barbara. We thought we had won the jackpot at the sight of two such gorgeous girls. We didn't hesitate to ask them to a dance being held the following evening. The girls politely accepted

Barbara and Jean.

and we decided to take our leave. As we were saying our goodnights, Jean and Barbara's father said to us, "If there is anything at all that you boys ever need, the car or a date with the girls, anything at all, all you've got to do is ask."

'We thanked them all for their hospitality and as we walked down the driveway, Noel turned to me and remarked, "Did you ever get an offer like that in your whole life?"

'Sadly, after the tour had ended and everyone was back in their own country, I heard that Barbara had died after what appears to have been a fairly minor abdominal operation. I did keep in touch with Jean, though, and we remain friends to this day.'

We could fill another book with anecdotes told by Noel Henderson, who also happens to be my uncle as he married Dad's sister Betty. Anyone who knew him was well aware of his fantastic sense of humour which could be a bit bold on occasion!

'Noel played a fair few pranks on me over the years and, in a spot of unintentional payback, I managed to get one back on him. On board ship, we were warned that because of the large amounts of laundry, there was a chance of catching a fungal infection which affected the groin area and was known as 'Dhobi itch'. Unfortunately, Noel caught it and as I was a medical student, he thought he would test my knowledge by asking me what the best treatment was. I advised him to get a treatment called Whitfield's Ointment. Noel applied it lavishly before going to bed.

'The next morning, I saw Noel at breakfast. "How did you sleep?" he asked.

'"Fine, thanks," I replied, wondering at his unusually sarcastic tone.

'"Lucky for you," Noel replied. "I spent the night in a cold bath as that damned ointment you recommended practically burned the skin right off my groin. I wouldn't take up dermatology as a speciality if I were you!"'

'He must have made the tour a lot of fun.'

'That's for sure. He was always having a joke, usually at your expense! Often in the hotels the team stopped in, two or three of us had to share a room. On one occasion, Noel and I were sharing a room comprising a double and a single bed. Noel began by saying how he found it very strange that two friends could easily fall out over the most trivial things and wasn't it sad and such a shame, and on he went. I agreed, but wondered what was coming, when

Noel continued to labour this point. He then went on to say, "So I am having the double and you are having the single!"

'I remember on another occasion on tour when I had taken a girl out the previous evening, Noel asked whether I had enjoyed my evening and how was the goodnight kiss. I was quite shy back then and replied that I hadn't kissed her goodnight; I had shaken hands with her because I had only just met her. Noel nearly had a fit, saying, "If it gets around that a member of the Lions is taking girls out and shaking hands with them at the end of a date, we'll be a laughing stock. Would you think of our reputation!"'

'What was that story about Noel making Taffy Davies go on a double date?' I asked.

'Oh, yes – when we were in the North Island, to be honest I can't remember exactly where, Noel met a girl and invited her out one evening. She said she would love to go, but unfortunately her mother was recently widowed and on her own and was finding it difficult to be left by herself. Noel, not to be thwarted, went back to the hotel, got hold of Taffy Davies, the Welsh masseur, who he figured at the age of sixty-two was probably around the same age as the mother, and told him to get dressed up as he had a date and he was going out with the mother. So Noel and Taffy double-dated that evening! That was Noel, he never took no for an answer!'

'I believe that your Lions team had quite a reputation for singing and were actually known as 'The Singing Lions' – is that true?'

'Yes. One of the features of the tour was the singing. The thirteen Welshmen could sing and we were moulded into quite a reasonable choir. Cliff Davies, a front-row forward, was the conductor and we sang numerous songs, many of them Welsh, such as 'Sosban Fach', a traditional Welsh folk song. Everywhere we went, we were asked to sing, and records were actually made before we left New Zealand. One of the songs that went down well after we'd been entertained at some of the many functions held for us was a song that began, "Goodnight ladies, goodnight ladies we're going to leave you now". I think it was by E.P. Christy and was an old song that dated back to the late 1800s.

'When we'd arrived in Wellington, Noel and I had bought an anthology of poetry, which we shared with some others on the tour. Dai Gent loved poetry and he, Noel and I would often sit and enjoy some poems from this book. On a railway trip to the South Island, Dai was looking through the book and to those of us in the same carriage he said, "Listen to this lads, it's beautiful." Thereupon he recited Thomas Love Peacock's poem 'Love and Age', which starts:

I play'd with you 'mid cowslips blowing
When I was six and you were four;

When garlands weaving, flower-balls throwing,
Were pleasures soon to please no more.
Through groves and meads, o'er grass and heather,
With little playmates, to and fro,
We wander'd hand in hand together;
But that was sixty years ago.

'I love that poem, I love the nostalgia of it. I would often quote this to you and Caleb; I particularly love the verse later on that reads:

How dearly words want power to show and my joy in
them was past expression.

'It is a beautiful poem that perfectly expresses the passage of time and how love changes and yet lasts no matter how much time may pass.

'After the tour was over, Dai published a piece about 'The Irish on Tour' [which is reprinted on page 107] after he returned to England, which emphasises Dai's delightful way of expressing himself.'

I know Dad is not going to talk about how highly he was praised on this tour, but, fortunately, there are enough accounts from other people that tell the story of Dad's time as a Lion.

He did himself proud – the *Rugby Almanack of New Zealand* named him one of their five Players of the Year and called him 'the outstanding genius of the British Isles side'. The other player who came from outside New Zealand, chosen as one of the top five from that year, was Welsh three-quarters Ken Jones, who was a wonderful runner; he had an exceptionally good rugby brain and had won a silver medal in the 4 x 100 metres relay at the 1948 Olympic Games. Dad told me how honoured he was to be chosen along with the other four players, as he appreciates how highly regarded New Zealand rugby is. The three New Zealanders who made up the five players of the year were Tiny White, Pat Crowley and Lester Harvey.

The 1951 *Rugby Almanack of New Zealand* wrote:

Kyle was primarily an excellent team man; faultless in his handling; able to send out lengthy and accurate passes, and adept at making play for his supports. The possessor of a neat side step; his instantaneous reacting, quick thinking and neat footwork enabled him to flash through the occasional opening in an elusive break that usually spelt danger. A feature of his play was his sturdy defence and solid tackling, whilst his kicking, either into a gap or defensively to touch, was snappy and accurate. The very fact that he was so often measured up as being in the class of A.E. Cooke and other stars of the past, indicates the impression he left behind – the complete footballer.

The bus in which we travelled around New Zealand.

His individual genius was an outstanding feature of the First Test too, and here again he was responsible for the two tries, scoring one himself when he gathered in a short clearing kick, flashed past the opposition and racing to the line outpaced the defence ... Jack Kyle has left a name that will ever live in the annals of New Zealand Rugby.

Getting back to the tour, Dad tells me about the first games.

'The first match of the tour was in Nelson, though I didn't play in it, and the Lions won on penalty kicks. A bus then took us through the Buller Gorge where we were frequently within a few feet of large drops into the gorge, which had some of the players feeling very nervous, myself included! The next two games were against Buller in Westport, which we won 24–9, and West Coast in Greymouth, which we won 32–3 – I scored three tries in

Training before the first match in Nelson.

that match. It was a wet day but I managed to hold on to the ball and I was able to find some large gaps in the defence and take advantage of them as well as the long passes from Rex Willis. At every game the ground was full to capacity as the New Zealanders were as mad about their rugby then as they are today – we got a great reception at every match. There was an emphasis on running rugby by the Lions, which I loved and made the matches much more enjoyable for me.'

A New Zealand journalist wrote about Dad's performance:

Kyle played brilliantly. Several times he cut the defence to ribbons with dazzling runs. He scored three tries, two of them with ridiculous ease.

When the team left Greymouth a hundred or so people came to see them off. The Mayor of Greymouth sent the following telegram to his counterpart in Dunedin:

Have just farewelled the British Isles rugby team. I commend them to you and the people of Dunedin as splendid ambassadors of Britain and a fine party of sportsmen.

'From there, we all travelled by train across the South Island for our match in Carisbrook in Dunedin against Otago, who were considered one of the strongest provinces. This game was a bit of a disaster, as we lost 23–9. I think we were not prepared for the speed, organisation and determination of the Otago team. I did score the only try for the Lions, which was small comfort. However, the New Zealand press were very fair to us and wrote that we did well to not lose the match by more points. All of the forwards playing for Otago had played for New Zealand and so had three of the backs. For any provincial side to beat the Lions was a tremendous feat. Even so, as Lions we always got a great reception as the spectators appreciated the style of open running rugby which we always tried to play. The day we played was absolutely beautiful and sunny and again there was a capacity crowd of about 35,000 people.'

'It sounds like once you got to Otago, the matches became much tougher,' I said.

'Yes, and worse was to follow. We travelled to Invercargill in the very south of the South Island, and lost 11–0 to Southland, a side that was not considered to be a top rugby province. George Norton broke his arm, which meant that we had lost our top place-kicker, which was a huge blow, as you have to remember that penalties had the same number of points as a try in those days.

The game at Invercargill was played on a Tuesday and the First Test was at Carisbrook in Dunedin on the following Saturday. Needless to say, with two defeats – one by a team that the Lions were supposed to have beaten easily – we were written off before we even set foot in Dunedin, and there was some criticism that we were not considered strong enough opposition for a New Zealand test side.

'I tried not to let this bother me too much. I was a great believer in taking it easy before a game and conserving my energy. I usually had a late breakfast and did not have any lunch. On the day of the First Test, the sun shone and I do recall some nerves taking hold an hour or so before kick-off. It was a large test ground which was packed and the crowd gave us a very warm welcome. We were without Bleddyn Williams due to injury, which was a blow, but Ivor Preece was put in the centre to partner Jack Matthews. It wasn't a very pretty game of rugby but fortunately, we redeemed ourselves and that match remains one of the highlights of my career, as I managed to score a good try. We drew the match nine points each.

'More times than I can recall, I have been asked what I think my most valuable try was, and I have to say I think it was that one against the All Blacks during that First Test. Such moments of inspiration as I managed then always happened at a subconscious level – and when the opportunity arose, I wasn't going to miss it, but at the time you are quite unaware of what you are doing. Sometimes I say it was as if the game was being played through you, which I know may sound a bit odd, but that is how it felt.'

According to the reports, it was a sensational try where Dad picked the ball up from a kick towards the left-hand touchline. He streaked into open play and away from Bob Scott, the New Zealand full-back, and wriggled free from the left-winger Nau Cherrington's grasp to place the ball over the line. This is how it was described by a journalist from *The New Zealand Post*:

He saw a gap, he slipped through it in a twinkling, he veered clear of the rocklike Scott with speed that left the latter seemingly immobile, and when his change of direction put him within Cherrington's grasp, he combined a sinuous wriggle with such spirited determination that he was able to plant the ball over the line.

After that try, *The Evening Post* also paid tribute to him:

It is doubtful whether one player will live longer in the memories of those who saw the 1950 Carisbrook test than Kyle. He scored a dazzling try which will always hold a place on Carisbrook's mythical rugby honours board.

'The second try we scored that day was from a cross-kick I made towards Ken Jones, who picked up the ball and put it down over the All Blacks line. Although we did not win any of our four test matches, we lost by very narrow margins, and to draw with the All Blacks was a very good result. We also won all of our remaining twenty-two provincial games, which were played over a period of three months. So following the First Test, pride was restored and indeed a new respect shown towards the Lions.'

'How did the Second Test go?'

'That game was played in Christchurch, at Lancaster Park. It was a fine day, but the ground was heavy from recent rain. There was a capacity crowd of 44,000 packed

Ken Jones being chased by Peter Henderson and Peter Johnstone
during the Third Test in Wellington.

into the stadium. Unfortunately it was a less successful affair, and we lost 8–0. The All Blacks started strongly and were dominant in all areas and although we made a few breaks, we were unable to break through the defence. We did receive praise from the New Zealand press, however, as they said we had done sterling work in preventing the All Blacks from scoring any further tries. The New Zealand forwards were dominant and they always fought so hard to obtain the ball, which was very challenging to play against.

'The Third Test in Wellington was played on 1 July, and we lost 6–3. There were provincial games midweek

Ron Elvidge scoring the only try of the Third Test in Wellington.

Kicking forward during the Third Test in Wellington.

and a game on Saturday in between the two final tests. Wellington had bad weather all that week, so again the ground was quite heavy, although on the day the rain had cleared but it remained overcast. There was a crowd of about 41,000 there. It was a close match and from what I remember there were quite a few injuries to the All Black pack. The All Black captain, Ron Elvidge, was badly injured but returned to the field of play with both a bad eye and an injury to his arm and managed to score the only try of the game, for which he has always been remembered because of his great courage.

'Before leaving Wellington, the Governor-General, Sir Bernard Freyberg VC, and Lady Freyberg held a reception for 250 guests at Government House. There were some past All Black players from 1924 and 1935 there and it was great to meet them.

'In between games, we had some time to relax and we were taken to various tourist attractions, such as a

Ginger Osborne and Karl Mullen during the reception at Government House.

traditional Maori ceremony, and many of the towns we visited hosted receptions for us in their local town hall and gave us tours of the area. We had a great day in Waitangi where we relaxed and had a picnic in glorious sunshine. Everywhere we went we were shown such great hospitality.

'The Fourth Test, played at Eden Park in Auckland on 29 July, was lost 8–11, but was considered one of the most thrilling games of the tour. Bob Scott, the New Zealand full-back, kicked a penalty, converted a try and dropped a goal. The Lions then replied with a try that was started from our twenty-five when the wing three-quarters threw the ball over the lineout – I caught the ball and passed it to Lewis Jones who was playing full-back and had come inside Bleddyn Williams, playing at

Playing a tour match against Auckland.

Peter Henderson on his way to score his try during the Fourth Test.

centre. Lewis Jones ran thirty or forty yards and the ever-watchful Ken Jones met up with him about the halfway line. Lewis Jones passed to Ken Jones who was chased by various New Zealand players, but, being the runner he was, they were not going to catch him. There are some wonderful photos of Ken running at full speed towards the All Blacks line.

'The final game of the New Zealand leg of the tour was in Wellington's Athletic Park where we beat the New Zealand Maoris, 14–9. The weather was beautiful and we were able to play flowing running rugby which seemed to enthral the crowd. During the game, Noel [Henderson] scored an impressive try, which was fully deserved and I was delighted for him.

'Between games we often visited schools and spoke at them and at other clubs. We also spent two nights in

*Downtime in New Zealand.
Opposite page: at Lake Rotorua
(top), Cook's Monument
(centre and bottom). This page:
an open-cast mine (top), Burgess
Park (centre) and Katopero
Dam (bottom).*

Kaiteriteri

Rotorua, where we were able to experience the Maori culture and learn some of their songs, and they performed a concert for us on our first night there. We also went to see the hot springs, a feature of the region, which also has many beautiful lakes.

'There were twenty-three games played over a period of three months in New Zealand and I played in seventeen of them, including the four test matches.'

'So how did the tour wrap up? Were you sad to leave New Zealand?'

'Leaving Wellington by ship for Sydney was an emotional experience, the crowd on the quayside sang "Now is the hour when we must say goodbye". There were streamers held aloft by those of us on board and those on land and gradually these broke as the ship pulled away. I

Leaving New Zealand, making our way through the crowds towards the ship.

loved my time in New Zealand. We received such a warm welcome wherever we went and the crowds were fantastic. Bill McKay and Don Hayward later returned to live there because they had enjoyed the country and its people so much during the tour.

'Crossing the Tasmin Sea from Wellington to Sydney turned out to be a very rough journey – at times there were very few people in the dining room for meals – and we arrived into Sydney half a day later than expected after four and a half days at sea. We spent a month playing rugby in Australia, including two tests – one in Brisbane, which we won 19–6, and one in Sydney, which we won 24–3. We also played a game against a Combined County XV in Canberra, but I didn't play in that game. The First

Test in Brisbane was played at the Cricket Ground and our full-back Lewis Jones had a wonderful game, scoring all eleven of our points in the first half. The Second Test in Sydney was played at Sydney Cricket Ground and we were able to take advantage of some mistakes in defence by the Australians. The Australian points were scored by the scrum-half Cyril Burke who was praised by the media afterwards for his play during the game.

'The social life during the tour of Australia was also lively, and as we were carefree and unattached, we frequently enjoyed meeting and going out with girls. I recall another double date during which Noel and I took two sisters to a nightclub. We ordered four drinks but had no idea how expensive they were going to be. After we had emptied our pockets and the girls had emptied their purses, we were still a bit short of the total to be paid, but we were able to come to an agreement with the manager – being in our Lions jackets may have helped our cause. We dashed out of the nightclub so the girls could catch the last tram home, but we were too late – much to the disgust of our dates, they had to take off their high heels as they walked the few miles home. When we received our expenses money which we were given on board, Noel and I reimbursed the girls but unfortunately I don't think we left a very good impression on that occasion.

'After our final game in Australia, we took the train from Sydney to Melbourne and we boarded our ship called the

Strathnaver to head home. We travelled back via various Australian ports and then headed out across the Indian Ocean. After nearly two weeks on board, we stopped in Colombo in Ceylon – as it was called then, it's now Sri Lanka – and played a game against a local side late on a very hot humid afternoon, which we won 44–6. Whilst we were playing, a polo match was going on in an adjacent field, it was all very colonial! The team had a bit of time to do some sightseeing after the game and we enjoyed a delicious dinner the evening before we left, which was hosted by the Ceylon Rugby Football Union in the Grand Oriental Hotel. It was a very relaxed affair and we went back to the ship which set sail soon after midnight and took us to Bombay, where we were also entertained by the local rugby union.

'The *Strathnaver* was a huge passenger ship, unlike the *Ceramic*, and there were over 1,000 people on board. Because the tour was over, there was no rugby training to be done or discussions to be had, and we had a very relaxing journey home, with the ship stopping at Aden and going through the Red Sea and the Suez Canal. We sailed through the Mediterranean, stopping at Marseilles, then sailed round the Bay of Biscay and finally on to London, from where the team all split up to go to their various home towns or cities. That tour constituted my first and only circumnavigation of the globe.

'I found out later that towards the end of our tour of New Zealand, a man called to the hotel where the Lions were staying. They told me he was bitterly disappointed when he heard that I was out, and said, "I just came to tell him that he's as good as Cookie."'

A.E. Cooke was the outstanding All Blacks three-quarter who played from 1924 to 1930 and, for rugby enthusiasts in New Zealand, the debate about who was considered the better player remains as divisive as ever.

The media and others often discuss comparisons between players. Cliff Morgan, the great Welsh out-half of the 1950s, in his generosity wrote to Dad and said that he believed Dad to be the better player. Dad replied and said that if you spoke to South African rugby pundits, they would talk about Cliff Morgan and his brilliant play during the 1955 Lions tour. Dad quoted a favourite line from a Yeats poem in the letter to Cliff: 'And I shall dine at Journey's end with Landor and with Donne.'

Dad told me this line expresses how honoured he felt, just to be thought good enough to sit down and dine with these other top rugby players.

'I arrived home from the Lions tour in early October, having been away for about six months. During the time I was playing rugby, there was a wonderful word called 'staleness', the general consensus of its meaning was that if you played too much rugby, you became mentally and physically tired – and, consequently, did not play well. So players were often given a few months off and a week off here and there during the season to avoid this 'staleness'.

Being greeted by my parents on my return home from the Lions tour.

For this reason, I played no rugby during the months of October and November but occasionally went with my father to watch a rugby match. My father knew very little about the game and was always full of questions, just as you have been, Justine, when we have gone to the odd international together!

'The tour was a wonderful experience. Aside from the great friendships I made and seeing all the wonderful new countries, I suppose the highlight with regards to the rugby would have to be the drawn First Test in Dunedin against the All Blacks on Saturday, 27 May 1950. Today, that would be hailed as a fantastic achievement and we probably wouldn't hear the end of it for months, but I suppose with time much of the memory of it has largely passed now.

'I also remember the great times I shared with Noel. When he died of bowel cancer in 1997, I mourned for a great friend and brother-in-law, who I had hoped to spend many more happy years with in our retirement.'

About a week before he died, Dad and I went up to see Noel, and Noel and Dad reminisced about their 1950 tour to New Zealand. They were talking about something that hadn't quite gone to plan when Noel spontaneously quoted the following:

It's easy to be happy when life goes along with a song.
But the man worthwhile is the man who can smile
When everything goes damn wrong.

Noel.

'That was Noel in a nutshell. He was always optimistic and when he became ill and knew that he was facing death, he was incredibly courageous. I miss him greatly. I spoke at his funeral and I was determined to give him a good send-off. It was important to me to do it well for Betty and the family. I quoted William Cory's 'Heraclitus':

They told me, Heraclitus, they told me you were dead,
They brought me bitter news to hear and bitter tears to
*   shed.*
I wept as I remember'd how often you and I
Had tired the sun with talking and sent him down the
*   sky.*
And now that thou art lying, my dear old Carian guest,
A handful of grey ashes, long, long ago at rest,
Still are thy pleasant voices, thy nightingales, awake;
For Death, he taketh all away, but them he cannot take.'

'I thought you spoke so beautifully to celebrate the life of your good friend and a wonderful man. I personally think it is the best I have ever heard you speak. Let's wrap up this chapter on a more cheerful note as Noel would have wanted it. What was that story Noel told you about the three ages of man?'

'Oh yes – he had so many funny stories and jokes, he could keep any party amused all evening. Noel told me the time he met a friend and said to him, "You're looking great." The friend replied, "Look here, Noel, as far as I am concerned, there are three ages of man – there's youth, there's middle age and there's, 'Damn it, you're looking great!'"'

Playing golf with Noel at Whangarei.

THE IRISH ON TOUR
A Personal Note
By
D.R. GENT (Gloucester and England)
Rugby Correspondent of *The Sunday Times*.

I am sure that everybody in the Rugby world was delighted when it was announced that J.A.E. Siggins has been appointed Manager of the British Isles touring side that will visit South Africa at the end of this season. It is an open secret that competition for this honour was very keen indeed in all four countries. But it is difficult to think of anybody better qualified for such a post than "Jack" Siggins, a great forward in his day, an excellent "mixer," and one who has kept closely in touch with the game since he gave up playing.

This office is no sinecure. It was my great good fortune to accompany the side that went to New Zealand in 1950. Never has a body of sportsmen so impressed the people of that country for their "sporting" approach to this great game as did the party that Surgeon-Captain L.B. Osborne, R.N, "managed" and Karl Mullen captained, and the Prime Minister of New Zealand, Mr. Sidney Holland, more than once bore testimony to this effect on public occasions. I was an intimate member of the party and it was a joy to be in such genial company, to watch the kind of football they played, and to sense the wholesomeness of the reaction of hosts and guests. The players themselves were a credit to the idea of sending touring sides to parts of the Commonwealth. But they themselves would be the first to say how helpful Captain Osborne's "managing" was, as well as the captaincy of Karl Mullen. New Zealand is one of the easiest countries in the Commonwealth to which to send a Rugby side, as everyone knows. But "Jack" Siggins, together with the captain who will be appointed to help him (another delicate appointment this), will make a happy event of this visit to South Africa and Rhodesia, I feel sure.

But I have chosen to write about the last touring side that we sent away mainly because I want to stress what a large part Irish players took in making the outing such a happy one, and upon the arrangements for Karl Mullen's men the Tours Committee will try to model the coming tour. Of the players (thirty to begin with, and augmented by another in the middle of the tour), nine were Irishmen, which included the captain: J.W. Kyle, J.S. McCarthy, J.W. McKay, Tom Clifford, N.H. Henderson, G.W. Norton, J.E. Nelson, and M.F. Lane were the others. A more cheery party within a party I have never seen.

First, there was Karl himself. Wherever we went, crowds from the neighbourhood came to greet us, and there were always speeches. Karl's smile and delightful brogue captivated everybody, and though he couldn't help talking sense, it didn't matter what he said – they just loved it! On the field, he was a magnificent leader, frail and pale though he looked. He has a way with him, as everyone knows, and he more than once induced me to come and speak to schools on the game with him, though my church is not his. Still, Karl and Jim McCarthy and I cheered them up, and the boys seemed to like the look of us, and especially the touring team captain. Lucky will the Tours Committee be to find such an attractive and tactful and competent leader this time again.

Then there was "Jack" Kyle, one of the outstanding players of the side, and though "Jack" has played some beautiful football "at home," he has never, I think, quite reached the heights he did out in New Zealand. Here is another man who can talk, and who loves to help, by his presence and his message, organisations of young people who are interested in Rugby Football (that is everybody in New Zealand!) and life generally, and are delighted to sit at the feet of sportsmen who are, and look like, the sort of people they want to copy. I won't say more about a Rugby man whom I admire, and whom I value as a great friend, and who bids fair to shine in his profession and to help tremendously in guiding young people along the road of wholesome endeavour.

Jack Kyle's close friend was Noel Henderson. Recently they have become closer friends, for, I believe, Noel has married Kyle's sister. On the way out, these two had the next cabin to me, and almost before we were clear of the Mersey on that tough Saturday afternoon (April 1), I heard melodious sounds of lovely Irish folk songs next door. At first they thought they were disturbing me. But I soon gave them plainly to understand that the only time I should bang the dividing partition would be when they stopped! To a Welshman, it was all sheer joy to listen to them. Big bluff Noel with a nice voice gave himself little respite in more robust activities, but Kyle used to find comfort when he was not singing aloud, in reading poetry with anthologies on hand all the time. Jimmy McCarthy, Tom Clifford and "Mick" Lane represented the South of Ireland, all in their own homely Irish manner: "Jimmy" bright and cheery, though with frequent visible signs of home sickness; "Tom" ever smiling, radiant with health and happiness, the countryman to perfection, a grand front-row forward, and "Mick," wistful and gentle, and withal a beautiful "wing" to watch when he has a fair chance to go for the corner, and he has had many more chances out there than he ever had at home! George Norton had the bad luck to break his arm in the fifth match of the tour, and was unable to play anymore. But he was always a splendid "party" man. Finally, there were "Bill" McKay and "Jimmy" Nelson. "Bill" one of the outstanding successes of the tour, on the field and off, and Jimmy Nelson slow to run into form, but magnificent when he did reach it. Yes, the Irish "boys" were splendid, and with the Welsh contingent, fourteen in number, naturally bore the brunt of the responsibility for the success of the team, on the field and off. Scotland with four players and England with three, being limited in a way by their numbers, though needless to say, most worthy "Lions," as the side was officially called.

I believe Ireland will again supply a fair number for the tour, for since the war, Irish football has been consistently good, attractive to watch and full of vigour and true Rugby spirit. I haven't seen any Irish Rugby this season yet, except in an exhibition game, as it were, between a side that the President of the Rugby Union (Mr W.C. Ramsay) got together on the first Saturday in September to play against the Wasps in London. On his side were, C.E. Pedlow, J. Hewitt and R.W. Thompson: they were outstanding, the backs, Pedlow, and Hewitt especially. Incidentally, the President's side was captained by Jack Matthews, the former Wales and Cardiff centre three-quarter, who has turned out the last season and this in this kind of game. He played at full back, and he as much as anybody helped to land his side home, after a delightful game by 24 points to 20. Once more, I hope many of the best Irish players will find themselves able and anxious and lucky enough to figure in the 1955 "Lions." Such a party needs its Irishmen, as they have shown in many previous tours, in Karl Mullen's side and

Sam Walker's (to South Africa in 1938) and Tom Smyth's (also to South Africa in 1910).

May I just add a short personal note? The years are rolling on, and soon, I shall keep a little further back from the game than I have since I went on the field in 1903 and came off it to write in 1913. Now I shall in the main read what others say and picture it all that way. But the memories will keep flooding in, I know, and among them will figure hosts of Irishmen, happy, colourful, generous, and warm-hearted, and many great Rugby names and games.

CHAPTER SIX

RUGBY MEMORIES FROM THE 1950s

'That time is past,
And all its aching joys are now no more,
And all its dizzy raptures. Not for this
Faint I, nor mourn nor murmur;
other gifts have followed.'
taken from 'Lines Written a Few Miles
above Tintern Abbey' by William Wordsworth

During my trips up to see Dad, I discovered a whole array of memorabilia and photographs contained within scrapbooks and letters. It is incredible how many items and books relating to rugby Dad has been sent over the years. As we looked back through some of them, I asked Dad to tell me about his rugby days in the early 1950s. Dad has a great memory, and the books and articles also help as reminders of a bygone era.

In 1951, Ireland had one of their best years in rugby, beating France, England and Scotland and drawing against Wales in Cardiff. As all games had to be won outright to win the Triple Crown or the Grand Slam, the Irish had to be content with winning the championship. I asked Dad what he remembers about that year.

❀

'Looking back on that game where Ireland missed a couple of penalties against Wales, we longed for the boot of George Norton, who was a fantastic place-kicker and I am sure he would have converted them. George was injured and unable to play at the time. Apart from a few games in 1954 when I was dropped from the Irish side, I played in every the Ireland games up to 1958.

'During the 1950s, although Ireland won several games, we never managed to win another Triple Crown or Grand Slam. I ended my international career in 1958 having gained forty-six international caps, a world record that I held until the 1990s.

'I suppose I should mention the two moments in my rugby career which have followed me throughout my lifetime and have never been forgotten by avid rugby fans. One was the try that I scored against France at Ravenhill in 1953, when I captained the Irish side and Jean Pratt

With French captain Jean Pratt before the 1953 championship match.

was French captain. I have to say that I don't remember much about the try itself. I know I dodged a few players and when I had the line in my sights, my only intention was to get there before being tackled. After the try, A.P. McWeeney wrote his famous lines published in the *Irish Independent*:

> *They seek him here, They seek him there*
> *Those Frenchies seek him everywhere*
> *That paragon of craft and guile*
> *That damned elusive Jackie Kyle.'*

'*Well as usual, Dad, you are being too modest. Let me refresh your memory about the try by quoting from McWeeney's match report:*

> *Kyle fielded a fly-kick to touch and catching the ball waist high on the twenty-five made tracks for the line. He feinted to pass to Mortell (11) outside him, but cut in and beat the entire French defence by an outstanding combination of strong running and sharp turning which caught the defence on the wrong foot. He plonked the ball down behind the posts without a hand being laid on him.*'

'Well, that sounds more impressive than I remember! The second incident I recall was the only time I ever scored a drop goal in international rugby. It was against Wales in

Scoring a try against France, Ravenhill, 1953.

1956, when Wales needed to beat Ireland to win a Triple Crown.

'The Welsh full-back kicked the ball towards the Irish touchline and I caught it before it went into touch. Someone in the crowd, no doubt thinking that I didn't know what to do, shouted at me to drop a goal. I heard the call and, for want of anything better to do, I kicked the ball and, to my surprise let alone the crowd's, the ball soared between the Welsh posts.

'In that game, Cecil Pedlow kicked a penalty for us and Marney Cunningham scored a try, which meant that Wales, who had thwarted us on many occasions, were denied their Triple Crown. In the newspapers the next day, at the end of the match report, they added the news that Marney Cunningham had entered the priesthood – he never played rugby for Ireland again. This was all the more unusual because we, his team-mates, had no idea that he had been about to make this life-changing decision.

'Another very significant event occurred in rugby in 1954 and, had it not been resolved, it could have led to Irish rugby being divided, which would have been catastrophic both for the sport of rugby and for Ireland.

'We were due to play Scotland at Ravenhill. The players from the Republic of Ireland told the IRFU president that they did not feel comfortable standing for the British national anthem. They were ordered to meet in a hotel room. Jim McCarthy knew that some of the players were even refusing to go out on to the pitch for the anthem. He persuaded them to see sense, and he reminded them their actions could divide Irish rugby into north and south, and that no one wanted that. It was a very significant moment. As it turned out, a shortened version of the anthem known as 'The Salute' was played and Ireland didn't play another international match at Ravenhill.'

I had never heard this story before – though at an event in the summer of 2013, we met Ronnie Kavanagh who confirmed Dad's account of what happened. He also mentioned that a couple of the Ulster boys were oblivious to the drama unfolding behind the scenes and thought the other lads were off in a room praying for the pope, who was ill at the time, and that when they got back on the coach to take them to the ground, one of them said to Jim something to the effect of, 'Sure, if you'd have told us you were off praying for the pope, we could have said a wee prayer for him too!'

'1958 was the first time Ireland beat a touring side, when we won against Australia at Lansdowne Road. The feature of this game was a remarkable try scored by Noel [Henderson] – he received the ball and ran from near the halfway line after receiving a pass from David Hewitt, whom I considered one of the greatest centres I ever played with. I also thought Noel was a great player and he did a lot of the hard work in defence.

'Tony O'Reilly frequently told the story of Noel

IRISH XV AGAINST AUSTRALIA

ing: Mr. A. Sanders (Touch Judge), J. A. Donaldson (Collegians), A. J. F. O'Reilly (Old Belvedere), P. J. O'Donoghue (Bec
rs), W. A. Mulcahy (University College, Dublin), J. B. Stevenson (Instonians), Mr. W. J. Evans (Referee). Seated: A.
w (C.I.Y.M.S.), N. Murphy (Cork Constitution), J. R. Kavanagh (Wanderers), N. J. Henderson (N.I.F.C.), Mr. W. E. Cr
(President I.R.F.U.), J. W. Kyle (N.I.F.C.), B. G. Wood (Garryowen), R. Dawson (Wanderers), P. J. Berkery (London Iri
On ground: D. Hewitt (Queen's University, Belfast), A. A. Mulligan (Cambridge University).

The team that beat Australia, 1958.

Noel Henderson scoring against Australia, 1958.

receiving the ball near the halfway line and setting off for the Australian line. At the same time, one of the photographers on the touchline packed up his camera to run to the goal line and was there behind the line to take a shot of Noel scoring the try. There is a remarkable photo of Noel going over the line, the Australian player is looking up at the sky as he was thrown on to his back by Noel as he tried to stop Noel from touching down.'

In 1953, Dad went on tour with Queen's University to British Columbia and California. A tour he recalls with much pleasure, both from a rugby-playing perspective and a socialising one, because he was with his friends from university. Queen's played five games in British Columbia and five in California. Although Dad had graduated in 1951, he was allowed to go along with his, by now, brother-in-law Noel Henderson, who had also graduated at that point, because they wanted to field a strong side. You were allowed to continue to play for the university for a year after you had graduated, and they were picked while still within this allowed condition.

'The tour was so enjoyable I guess because we were young and free-spirited and, for me, it provided another opportunity to visit a country I had never seen before. You have to remember that life was hard in Ireland during the 1950s. Most people did not have the opportunity to travel abroad. We were exceptionally lucky. I remember how we travelled, a four-engine plane came across from

Scotland and it took us to Newfoundland and then went on to Vancouver. Harry McKibbin was the manager and there were about thirty of us. The first game was against a Vancouver side and we were losing about ten points to five at half-time. This was due in no small part to a number of the players being somewhat distracted by a group of cheerleaders who were standing pitch-side. So at half-time, we were given a strongly worded reminder that in no uncertain terms were we to be looking at the glamorous line of girls waving their pom-poms, but we better put our focus back on the game. Fortunately, we managed to tear our eyes away and win.

'What I recall most about the tour is being put up in fraternity houses in the Canadian and American universities. When we stayed at Stanford University, Noel and I were staying in a room belonging to Gary Crosbie, Bing Crosbie's son. I remember when we entered the room, we stood with our mouths agape staring at Gary Crosbie's guitar sitting in the corner, but we dared not touch it.

'In Los Angeles we were caught up in the 'Spring Sing', which was a singing competition at UCLA, in which all the sorority and fraternity houses took part and which took place at the Pasadena Rose Bowl. One of the gentlemen roped our Queen's tour into singing at the interval. This was not a great experience for me, as I have no talent for singing whatsoever. Luckily there were enough good voices, so I was able to just pretend I was singing and mime the words! It was a great experience listening to these fine singers and Noel and I used to listen to a first-class quartet at the fraternity house practising the song 'Up the Lazy River' – it became a favourite of Noel's.

'I also remember we played at a huge stadium in Los Angeles where we were made to run out individually on to the pitch after a short bio on each player was given over the loudspeaker system, the way they do in American football. We had never in our lives seen a stadium of this magnitude and to hear your name resounding around it was very strange. The crowd were going mad and there was so much hype and noise. We couldn't understand what all the fuss was about.

'I also remember how unique the fraternity and sorority houses were. One of the girls told me they were essentially there to find a good husband and that if you were in a good sorority, your chances were well improved. I have never seen so many attractive-looking girls in one place before or since.

'After that tour, I returned home and continued to play rugby, whilst also continuing my training to become a consultant surgeon. During the 1950s, I had various jobs to do for my medical training. I was an extern house surgeon at the Royal Victoria where I continued my surgical training under various different surgeons. In 1954, I worked in the Queen's Anatomy Department teaching the students. I also did a surgical course in Edinburgh for three months in the late 1950s, which I really enjoyed, mainly as it coincided with the Edinburgh Festival where I was able to go and see some very good plays and other events. I stayed in a small boarding house on the Dalkeith Road. Edinburgh is a beautiful city and I had a great time while I was there.

'I also continued to play rugby for Ulster during the 1950s and I remember in particular when we drew with the All Blacks in January 1954 at Ravenhill. We were winning the match 5–0 at half-time but the All Blacks scored a try in the second half so we drew the match 5–5 and our forwards put in a great performance, particularly Jimmy Nelson.

'In 1958, I played a few games of rugby, but at the age of thirty-two I was not the player I had been ten years earlier, and I was consequently dropped from the side. After one game, Ernie Crawford, who was one of the Irish selectors and had played full-back for Ireland in the 1920s, came to me and told me that I was to stand up and announce my retirement at a rugby dinner that evening, but I didn't want to do that, it was not my way. I had enjoyed a remarkable rugby career, and I did not mind people knowing I had been dropped from the side. My time was over. I felt it was dishonest to stand up and say I was retiring because everyone knew my days were numbered anyway.'

After Dad finished playing international rugby, he was

Getting ready for training, 1958.

still a member of North Rugby Club and the captain of the Third XV – Brian Fitzgerald asked Dad if he would play for them. Although he was not very enthusiastic, he agreed to play at full-back. He certainly did not like having to tackle and go down on the ball, which he had seldom done during his rugby career. The year he played for the team, they won the Harden Cup. Dad often remarks on the friendships that rugby engenders – when he was home on leave from Africa, members of that winning Harden Cup side would get together and celebrate their success during the year Dad played with them. It was as important to them as winning a Grand Slam and I think it speaks for itself that Dad was a happy participant both in the team and at their annual reunion dinners.

Before Dad left Ireland for Indonesia in 1962, Charlie Freer (who was the Head of Sport at the BBC and a very good friend) contacted some of his rugby friends and other contacts and asked if they would like to contribute to getting Dad's portrait painted, to which they all agreed. They commissioned a very good artist called Taylor Carson, who had been a war artist for the United States Air Force in Northern Ireland from 1943 to 1945. Following his work during the war, he established himself as a portrait painter and is best known for his character studies. Dad was delighted to have his portrait painted. Taylor Carson duly arrived at the bungalow in Lambeg, where my parents lived at that time, and choosing the kitchen, where the light was best, sat Dad down at a table and began to paint. Dad was painted wearing his green rugby jersey and the portrait now hangs in Ravenhill. It used to hang in the offices there, but now it is to go into the new museum that is being built at the ground.

'How did you feel about having your portrait painted and did you like the outcome?'

'Many people said the portrait was not that like me, but I used to say, "If I wanted a likeness I would have got a photograph." I was very happy with it. I felt that Taylor Carson had captured a certain faraway look that I knew I often showed and I felt that the artist had a certain insight into the angle that he wanted to paint. I think he captured this hazy, dreamy look very well.'

When discussing the portrait, Dad told me the story of Graham Sutherland who had painted a portrait of Winston Churchill. Apparently Churchill hated it and said it must have been an example of modern art. The portrait was therefore put out of sight and never hung up. On his death, Churchill's wife destroyed the portrait. Dad felt this was a sad story, because if you permit yourself to be painted by an artist, you have to accept how he sees you and recognise that others may see a trait or a characteristic in us that perhaps we do not see in ourselves.

As we finish discussing Dad's rugby memories, I ask him about many of the friendships he has formed through rugby.

'One of the great joys that come from playing a team sport are the friendships made, which often last a lifetime. I have been very fortunate to make some great friends through the game and have shared amazing experiences with the guys on the Lions tour as well as many other tours and shared games together.

'We are exceedingly fortunate that rugby is united in Ireland and it was very important to me, as I wanted to be able to play with people from both the North and the South of Ireland. As you know, it has never mattered one bit to me where someone comes from or what their religion is. I am interested in people. Sport does forge strong bonds and I would imagine that is even truer today, as the players have to spend even more time in each other's company than we did in our day. We were freer to relax and enjoy the friendships we made through rugby. There wasn't too much competitiveness or rivalry, with it being an amateur sport.

'I remember my sister Betty being very cross with me, because when Noel was first courting her, I told Noel that if things didn't work out with Betty, I did not want it to affect our friendship and I hoped we would still remain friends!

'Noel was a great character and an excellent rugby player and although we were very different in many ways, I think that is part of the reason we got along so well. He brought me out of myself and made me join in sometimes when I might have been a bit reluctant. He made every occasion a joyful one and always brightened proceedings when you were in his company. He also had a very good singing voice and he would often sing a lovely rendition of 'Carrickfergus', one of his favourite songs. He was a very amusing man, but we also shared a love of reading and he liked a bit of poetry too on occasion. To think I probably would never have met him if I didn't play rugby makes me even more grateful to the game.

'We have already mentioned Cliff Morgan, who was another great character and an exceptional rugby player, admired all over Wales and beyond. Anytime I was in his company, I enjoyed myself thoroughly and it was always stimulating and interesting. He was a gifted raconteur and I feel very blessed to have known him.'

Cliff Morgan.

One weekend, I was up at Dad's and, after dinner, we sat down to watch some TV. I wasn't much interested in whatever was on and, as I sometimes do, I began to study Dad's bookshelves as I always find some treasure or another I haven't seen before. My eyes happened upon a volume of poetry by Yeats. I wouldn't be nearly as big a fan of poetry as Dad, but wanted to find a particular Yeats poem. As I pulled the book from the shelf, a folded piece of paper fell out. I unfolded it and discovered it was a letter that Dad had written to Cliff Morgan. Dad sometimes used to write out a letter in rough before he wrote it out properly and this was a draft copy. I had an eerie feeling that I was meant to find it. Dad was happy for me to read it and, as soon as I had finished, I knew it was meant for the book.

It was written on 25 April 2005, when Cliff was receiving treatment for the cancer of his vocal cords.

Dear Cliff,

Mary has told me that you have finished your x-ray therapy, that you are back home, and above all that you are in good heart.

When reading a book about Yeats, I came across this paragraph, and I hope you don't mind me sending it to you.

In the period between writing 'Sailing to Byzantium' and 'Byzantium', Yeats was very ill and after he recovered, he turned again to Blake, quoting particularly a letter of Blake's, written to his friend, George Cumberland Junior: 'I have been very near the gates of death, and have returned very weak and an old man feeble and tottering, but not in Spirit and Life, not in the real man, the Imagination which liveth for ever. In that I am stronger and stronger, as this foolish body decays.'

Yeats was immensely moved by this letter, describing it as 'the most beautiful of all letters'.

Obviously he found a physical parallel between his own life and Blake's, as also he had always found a likeness in Blake's thought. He saw him as the champion of the soul, fighting the mechanistic, abstract thought of Locke and Newton:

> *'Beating upon the wall*
> *Till truth obeyed his call.'*

We had a reunion of our 1948 Grand Slam side in County Kildare a few weeks ago, arranged by a small rugby club, Newbridge. There were nine of us, including Karl Mullen, Des O'Brien, Jim McCarthy and Jimmy Nelson. Had a delightful evening and, on the Sunday, Des had arranged for some of us to have lunch at Clongowes School. Before lunch, we all went to mass, including the Ulster Protestants! Don't remember everything the priest said in his address, but I do remember him saying:

'We should try to look on the past with gratitude, on the present with enthusiasm and on the future with confidence.'

I am just passing on these few thoughts Cliff, as I think of you.

Love and best wishes to you and Pat.
Jack.

'We have already discussed many of the friends I made through rugby, like Karl Mullen, Jim McCarthy, Bill McKay and many of the guys I went on the Lions tour with. I am very fortunate to say there are many other friends I could mention, including some of the men I played with from Ulster, such as Cecil Pedlow and Jimmy

Ireland's great back row trio, with whom I became great friends (l–r):
Bill McKay, Des O'Brien and Jim McCarthy.

Nelson, and there have been many other rugby players I have had the privilege to know down through the years.

Willie John McBride is also a good friend. We have been co-presidents of the Wooden Spoon Society together and I enjoy his company very much.

'Although I was finishing my rugby career as Tony O'Reilly was starting his, he has always been incredibly generous to me and has invited me to many social occasions.'

'I remember you going to his daughter's wedding in Mozambique. That must have really been something special.'

'It was indeed. I was in Zambia at the time, so didn't have too far to travel. It was held on Benguerra Island, one of four large islands that make up the Bazaruto Archipelago, off the coast of Mozambique. We were beautifully entertained for four days, it was a glorious location and I met a lot of interesting people. Tony has always been an incredibly generous friend and I don't mean just in a material sense. He is generous with his time and he is very thoughtful. Thanks to Tony, I have attended the World Cup in France and been invited to many rugby events and other social occasions. I remember Tony had special blazers made for us all when we went to the 2007 World Cup in France. Tony told us to send our measurements to Peter Kinnemonth, who was organising everything. Tony used to joke and say, "There's nothing Peter enjoys more than spending my money!" I have enjoyed many pleasant evenings and outings in Tony's company and he is a friend I hold in the highest regard. Perhaps I haven't always kept in touch with him as much as I should have, as I know he has such a busy life – I always felt more comfortable just dropping him the odd note, or enjoying his company when I was invited along.

'Someone else I would like to mention is Ollie Campbell. Ollie is one of life's gentlemen and he has always been very kind to me and very good at keeping in touch, both by phone and email. I remember he told me that Bob Scott, the great New Zealand full-back, whom I played against during the 1950 tour, had been very kind to him when he was playing rugby, and when I was going to New Zealand on a trip, Ollie gave me Bob's number. I called Bob when I was there and had a long chat with him. It was very special for me to be able to do that and I am grateful to Ollie for passing on his number.'

'I totally agree,' I said. 'I remember once I went to the internationals tent with you after a Six Nations match. As usual, you were whisked away to talk to lots of different people and I was left standing alone like a spare part. Ollie came over to me and spent lots of time talking to me and asking me about myself. When he came over, I said I was fine and was well used to this, but he was sincerely kind and treated me like an individual and not "Jack's daughter" and for that I will always think highly of him.'

'Yes, that sounds just like the man. I have been so lucky

in Ireland to meet so many good men through rugby and so many characters as well. I know there are many I have omitted to mention, so I hope they will forgive me if that is the case; the memory at eighty-eight is not quite what it was.

'Players understandably can often find it very difficult to adjust when they have to retire from rugby, as they lose the daily camaraderie that is part of being a team. However, in time they adapt and they should feel blessed they have enjoyed a career playing a sport they love and know they have made friendships for life in some cases. I am very grateful to the game of rugby for enriching my life so much in this way.'

CHAPTER SEVEN

SHIRLEY

'Tread softly because you tread upon my dreams.'
'Aedh Wishes for the Cloths of Heaven' by W.B. Yeats

As the months go by, Dad and I fall into a routine about how we work on the book. On a Friday evening, we chat about the part of Dad's life we are going to discuss over the weekend. Then, on Saturday morning, I ask a few questions to start him off and we take it from there.

Dad raises the subject of my mum and says it is important that we talk about her. This is an emotive topic for both of us, but I am glad he has brought it up and I am pleased he is willing to share his memories.

❀

'I met your mother in 1956, when I was thirty and she was twenty-two. She was working in the library at Queen's at the time, having completed a law degree at the university.

I sometimes studied at the university's library and one evening when driving home in my father's car, I spotted Shirley at the bus stop at the back of Queen's and offered her a lift into town, from where she was going to take a train or a bus to her home in Lisburn. She was a very attractive woman, and I was delighted when she agreed to go out with me. We went out on several dates and then got engaged. I remember her being a bit put out when I said that the wedding couldn't take place during the rugby season, but she relented and we were married in May 1957.

'Shirley was a very glamorous, outgoing and fun person. She loved company and hosting dinner parties. She also loved travel and we had some fantastic adventures together, going to the South of France many times, as well as moving abroad when I got my positions as a consultant surgeon.

'She was not particularly interested in my rugby career, but she did come and watch me in a few games. As my international career ended in 1958, she didn't have to put up with my rugby playing for too long anyway, but I don't think she minded too much either way.

'After a few years of marriage, Shirley manifested signs of bipolar disorder which, at that time, was known as Manic Depressive Psychosis. There are many degrees of this condition, and many people who do not suffer from the extreme manifestations of it often lead normal and

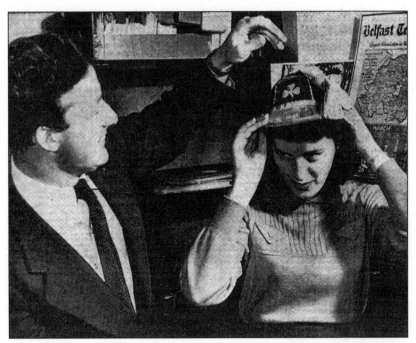

Shirley trying on one of my caps from 1957 shortly before we got married.

Marrying Shirley, May 1957.

controlled lives. Unfortunately, Shirley often manifested the extreme highs and lows of the illness. Her behaviour was very erratic, and it was very difficult to deal with on occasion.

'When we were living in Zambia, after I got a consultant position there in the mid-1960s, a male friend, who was on his own, often came to our house and dined with us in the evening. I was glad of this because I was frequently called out on emergency surgeries at night and I was glad that Shirley was not left alone. Unfortunately, spending such a lot of time together led to a relationship developing, which the friend was only too happy to encourage. I used to say that this old friend believed he was a knight in shining armour rescuing Shirley from a husband who didn't care about her.

'I initially tolerated this situation, believing that it was only a temporary relationship which would end when Shirley realised that she was better off with me than with this so-called friend. However, after a couple of unfortunate incidents, which I would rather not go into, I knew that I had no option but to seek a divorce.

'Shirley and her new partner did not contest the divorce and I was granted a decree nisi by the judge in Ndola in Zambia. At the divorce proceedings, I have always been extremely grateful to three people who came to court and testified on my behalf as to why I should be granted a divorce. However, the main problem was who was to have custody of Caleb, who was six, and you – you were only two at the time.

'Custody of children is not decided at the divorce proceedings but instead they are discussed in private in a judge's chambers with each side stating the reasons why they should be given custody. I was extremely worried that Shirley and my so-called friend would get custody of you and Caleb, as I felt that even if my influence was not the very best, I would rather that it was me looking after you than Shirley and her new partner, for whom I had lost all respect.

'I recall being in the operating theatre at North Hospital in Chingola and answering the phone when my solicitor informed me that I had been given custody. I can tell you, the relief was immense, as I had not been at all certain that I would actually be granted custody, as it is more common for custody to be given to the mother. The judge in giving me custody did tell me that it was not his usual custom to give custody to the father, and especially a busy professional, but in the present circumstances, he felt that you two should remain in our home in Chingola with reasonable access being granted to your mother. He did mention that there was a possibility of the custody agreement being reviewed in a year, but that didn't happen, as by then you and Caleb were well settled with me and your mother was used to the arrangement. At the time, your mother asked for a further discussion about custody being given to her and her now husband, but I refused to countenance this.

'I did not wish to deprive you and Caleb of your mother, though, my only wish was that you be safely looked after at all times, and I allowed her to see you both every weekend, which was more time than I had to give her under the court agreement.

'I had some happy times with your mother and I loved her very much when I married her. The tragedy of your mum's life was that she showed such potential, but was never able to fulfil it, and the illness was partly the cause.

'I have known many cases of people who have been deserted by their partner and have blamed themselves. I have had many men and women come to me to talk over their problems and many of them were left totally heartbroken. I always find this so sad and pointless in a way. I always said to those people that they needed to keep telling themselves that it wasn't their fault, that they had done the best they could, and that if their husband or wife had left them, then it was most definitely their spouse's loss. No one has a right to destroy your happiness. Whatever people do, they should not let their life be destroyed by a relationship breaking down. A poem that sums up exactly what I mean is Rupert Brooks' poem 'Desertion':

So light we were, so right we were, so fair faith shone,
And the way was laid so certainly, that, when I'd gone,
What dumb thing looked up at you? Was it something
    heard,
Or a sudden cry, that meekly and without a word
You broke the faith, and strangely, weakly, slipped
    apart.
You gave in, you, the proud of heart, unbowed of heart!
Was this, friend, the end of all that we could do?
And have you found the best for you, the rest for you?
Did you learn so suddenly (and I not by!)
Some whispered story, that stole the glory from the sky,
And ended all the splendid dream, and made you go
So dully from the fight we know, the light we know?

O faithless! the faith remains, and I must pass
Gay down the way, and on alone. Under the grass
You wait; the breeze moves in the trees, and stirs, and
    calls,
And covers you with white petals, with light petals.
There it shall crumble, frail and fair, under the sun,
O little heart, your brittle heart; till day be done,
And the shadows gather, falling light, and, white with
    dew,
Whisper, and weep; and creep to you. Good sleep to
    you!

'I have always found that music and poetry have given me strength during difficult times. The key to all of this is to realise your own self-worth. As I always said to those suffering in this way, "You are entitled to your place in the sun."'

I can see that talking about my mum has been an emotional experience for Dad, so I wrap up the conversation and give him time to relax. Dad never remarried and whilst I sometimes think that is a bit sad, I fully understand the reasons why he never wanted to. He has often said there is a certain selfishness being on your own, as you don't have to refer to anyone else about what you want to do or where you want to go. I know he is a man who enjoys peace and quiet, time to read and to reflect, and he never minded being on his own. He has certainly enjoyed the company of women over the years, but has never wanted to settle down again. It was also easier for my brother and me that Dad did not introduce a step-mother into our lives, which enabled us to have a much closer relationship with him. We would not have objected at all, of course, but we knew he was always very much his own man – his personal life was never any of our business anyway.

My parents were married for over ten years and shared many happy times together. Sadly, my mother's bipolar status clearly brought problems to the marriage. There were difficult times and anyone who has lived with someone who suffers from this illness will understand the difficulties.

My mother and her second husband went to live in Devon but, as my father had predicted, the relationship did not last and after a few years, her new husband sent my mother back to Ireland with ten thousand pounds. She was then looked after by her sister Jill and the Northern Ireland Health Authorities.

My mother died from aspiration pneumonia in April 2009 at the age of seventy-five. As Dad said, I think the sadness of my mother's life was what might have been, as she was a very intelligent woman but was never able to fulfil her potential. She and Dad rarely saw each other after their divorce but when they did, it was always very amicable and they still cared about each other and both of them would often ask Caleb and me how the other was doing. Caleb and I maintained a relationship with our mother throughout her life and although there were tough times, we also shared many happy occasions together.

Following this conversation about my mum, Dad asked me what it had been like to be brought up in a one-parent family. I cannot claim that it was easy not having a mother around much when I was growing up, but what I can say for sure is, it was an awful lot easier than living with parents who were fighting all of the time. I cannot ever remember my parents fighting, because my mother left when I was still a baby, but I do think it is much better for a child to be in a stable environment with one parent than to be in a fraught home with two parents who are both unhappy.

Dad ensured that we had a routine and life was kept as normal and secure for us as possible. Whilst I suppose I must have felt that my situation was somewhat unique, I don't ever remember feeling in any way traumatised, afraid or unhappy, and I have no doubt that was down to the stability that Dad provided for us. He also told me that he clearly remembers a psychologist once saying to him that one of the most important aspects of a child's life is to have the fun and enjoyment that being with other children brings, and we certainly had no shortage of fun in Zambia, because of the many friends we had and the easy-going lifestyle.

Every single family in the world has its issues and whether you are in a one-parent family or a traditional mum-and-dad scenario, what matters is that you feel loved and we certainly received plenty of that from both our parents.

We received incredible support from my extended family back in Northern Ireland too. My Aunty Betty and Uncle Noel looked after us while we were at boarding school, and having four grown-up daughters of their own meant that my aunt effectively continued her parenting by looking after us. She was fantastic. She sewed on name tags and organised everything that being at boarding school entails. My other aunts and my Uncle Eric also looked after us on occasion, as did all my cousins, so we were very much part of a tribe and that certainly made a huge difference.

CHAPTER EIGHT

A LIFE ABROAD

'All life is an experiment.
The more experiments you make the better.'
Ralph Waldo Emerson

As winter turned slowly to spring, I continued my trips up the M1 to Bryansford. The next part of Dad's life we covered was his decision to live abroad. I was looking forward to hearing about this time in his life. There was so much to discuss that it took a further three visits before we had exhausted all there was to talk about in relation to his travels.

I began by asking him where he got his love of travel.

❧

'I have always loved seeing new places and it doesn't matter where they are in the world, the further away, the better.

I also think I have always been quite independent. One day, at the tender age of four, I decided that I wanted to visit my grandparents, who lived about two miles from our house. I told no one of my plans and set off, knowing exactly how to find their house. When my grandmother opened the door to find me standing there, she had such a look of surprise on her face and, apparently, I calmly told her that I had come for a visit. My own mother was frantic by this stage, wondering where I had gone, and was both shocked and delighted when my grandmother arrived back to our house with me. I was oblivious to the commotion I had caused, but I like to think that I loved going places even at that age and perhaps this spirit of independence has stayed with me ever since.'

'So you had an independent spirit from an early age, but moving abroad must have been a very big decision.'

'Deciding to live abroad, in quite remote parts of the world, wasn't as difficult a decision to make as you'd expect. Aside from my interest in different cultures, I always felt I wanted to broaden my surgical horizons – I suppose I was influenced by the writings of Albert Schweitzer. I remember when the Lions were leaving Sydney in Australia, I knew we were going to be on board ship for a month going home and I wanted to ensure I had a good book to get stuck into, to help the journey pass more quickly. I went to a bookshop and bought a book by Schweitzer entitled *My Life and Thought*.

I had already read two of his books – *On the Edge of the Primeval Forest* and *More from the Primeval Forest* – and although there were several reasons why I wanted to work abroad, I must admit that reading these books probably played some small part in my decision. I also felt that my particular talents as a surgeon were more suited to working abroad, as I felt I could make more of a contribution in a developing country.

'I left Northern Ireland twice, once to go to Indonesia and the second time to go to Zambia. This desire to leave Northern Ireland was in part prompted by a desire to escape the level of recognition I had and my reputation as a rugby player – I wanted to be seen as a surgeon first and foremost and not as a rugby player who happened to be doing surgery. For someone seeking freedom, there is nothing like travelling to Africa or Asia for a bit of peace and quiet. I was able to escape the committees and functions – abroad, I was just Mr Kyle, the surgeon. It was very important to me that my life was not defined by my rugby career. This point was beautifully illustrated by a lady called Peggy Lawton. She was having a consultation with the Chief Medical Officer [CMO] Dr Tomlinson in Chingola, and Dr Tomlinson was telling her that the new surgeon had played rugby for Ireland, the Barbarians and the Lions, to which she replied: "Dr Tomlinson, I think if some of us were waiting on a trolley to go into surgery, we would be much more interested in what sort of a surgeon

Dr Kyle was, rather than how many times he had played rugby for Ireland."

'When I heard that, I was delighted and I admired her for her honesty, as that was exactly the point which I wanted to make, but could not say out loud.

'When I achieved my FRCS, I had already decided that I wanted to work abroad. In 1962, I applied for a job with the Standard Oil Company of New Jersey as a consultant surgeon based in Sumatra in Indonesia. Shirley was happy to go, as she enjoyed discovering new places, and as we had been surviving on my very meagre salary and this was a consultant position with a salary to match, she was happy that she would be enjoying a more comfortable lifestyle. I went to London for an interview and was put up in a hotel. They laid on a very lavish dinner for me. I had asked Jack Balmer, for whom I had worked in a hospital in Lurgan, for a reference, and it must have been a good one because I was offered the job.

'I didn't fly out to Indonesia for another three months, but the company paid me three quarters of my salary in the meantime, which was a great bonus. I remember spending two weeks in Oxford at an induction to prepare us for the different culture of Indonesia. We learned the basics of the language, some information about the local customs, how to greet people and any required etiquette. I decided I would bring some good surgical books with me to be prepared for any surgery I may not have encountered before.

'For the journey to Indonesia, I flew out first class with Air India, along with two nurses who were also starting work in the same hospital as me. One of them, Margaret, became a very good friend to Shirley. Shirley didn't fly out with me, but came out a few weeks later. It always took her a bit more time to get packed up and say her goodbyes to everyone – I couldn't wait because I had to start my job. On the way out, we had a stopover in Singapore and I was put up in the famous Raffles Hotel. I loved it because both Somerset Maugham and Ernest Hemingway had stayed there, two writers I love to read.'

This prompted a memory of my own. 'I remember you insisting I visit Raffles when I was returning from Australia once, via Singapore. I paid premium price for the pleasure of having a Singapore Sling in the famous Long Bar – though it was worth every cent! As you always say, "A little gracious living now and again is good for the soul."'

'Indeed. I am a firm believer in that! Also, it would be a waste to be in Singapore and not visit Raffles!

'The company had given us a basic overview of what our lives in Indonesia would be like and we were advised to do some shopping in Singapore, in order to equip ourselves with the necessary clothes and goods that we'd need in Sumatra, such as good rainproof gear and clothes for the hot weather, as well as any luxuries that we may not be able to buy in Indonesia, such as medicines, toiletries and any creature comforts we wanted.

'I had some aspirations to improve my golf and so one of the things I bought was a new set of clubs – even though they weren't on the list. I also sought out some wonderful tailors, who were recommended by the company. I bought several suits, which were beautifully made and excellent value, to help me cope with the Sumatran climate.

'From Singapore we flew to Jakarta. When Shirley came out, she told me that on her flight out to Singapore, everyone on board had been handed a packet of 'shark chaser' which they were told to sprinkle in the sea if the plane went down. As she was already afraid of flying, this did nothing to ease her fears!

'When we arrived in Indonesia, I was sent up to central Sumatra to a settlement called Pendopo. It was a very isolated spot with only about twenty families living there, all of whom were American, except for a British couple, Dr and Mrs Scott.

'As far as my surgical duties were concerned, the surgery in Pendopo was not particularly strenuous, and I don't remember being in any way overstretched or challenged.

'One of our more surreal experiences in Pendopo was being told that there was a man-eating tiger on the loose. It had killed twenty-seven people and everyone in the area was absolutely terrified. We had only been in the area for a few months and it was grim beyond belief, the thought of this tiger being able to pounce on people at random. As tigers are, it was very cunning and intelligent, and killed people by creeping up behind them and attacking them before they knew what was happening. Eventually the government sent specialists from Jakarta to catch the tiger and they trapped it by sacrificing a goat that was put in a cage into which the tiger walked.

'On another occasion, Shirley and I took a holiday to Hong Kong. As I passed through passport control, the immigration officer, who happened to play rugby, recognised my name and photograph. That evening, I received a call from the president of the Hong Kong Rugby Club inviting us to go to a function at the club. I went alone – Shirley was tired and didn't feel like going. Following a very enjoyable evening, the folk from the rugby club provided ongoing hospitality and invitations to us during our holiday. I guess it doesn't matter where you go in the world, rugby clubs are very hospitable and sociable.

'After I had spent six months in Pendopo, I was transferred to a hospital at Palembang, about 150 kilometres to the northeast. It was the capital city of Southern Sumatra and much larger than Pendopo. Palembang is the seventh largest city in Indonesia and also one of the oldest, dating back to the seventh century. We spent two years in Palembang, and whilst there wasn't a huge variety of surgery, I became an expert at removing stones from the kidney, ureter and bladder, as there were a lot of problems of dehydration because of the climate.

The leper colony in Palembang, Indonesia, 1962.

'One of my abiding memories of Indonesia is of a young girl in Palembang. There was a leper colony in the city and I, along with some of the other British doctors, would go down there to give them clothes and shoes, which had been provided by the local American community, and see if there was anything we could do to help. It was run by the Salvation Army, who did an incredible job there.

'On one visit, we noticed a little girl of about twelve who had leprosy in the toes of one of her feet. If you had leprosy, you were not allowed to leave the colony and so you were separated from your family, which was obviously very painful, especially for children. I decided we could do something for this little girl and so without asking permission, as we probably would not have been allowed to take her out of the leper colony, we quietly took her to the hospital and I did what was known as a fore-foot amputation. This is where we amputated the toes that were affected by leprosy. Following the operation, we were able to give her a special boot filled with cotton wool, so that she was able to walk without any difficulty.

'The upshot of the operation was that this little scrap of a girl was now free of leprosy and so she was able to go home and rejoin her family. She wrote me a beautiful letter telling me how thankful she was for what I had done for her and it touched me deeply. I cannot imagine how difficult it must have been for a twelve-year-old girl to be separated from her family, with no knowledge of whether she may ever see them again or not, and I was delighted to have been able to help her.

'One of the most enduring memories I have of my time in Indonesia is a holiday to Bali that your mum and I went on with the Scotts, the British couple from Pendopo.

'When we were there, we witnessed a magnificent festival in honour of the volcano Gunung Agung, whose name means 'Great Mountain', which sits at 3,014 metres. It had erupted in February 1963 not long after we arrived in Sumatra and approximately 1,600 people lost their lives and many thousands were left homeless. The Balinese take the volcano very seriously and honour it with prayers and shrines. The mother temple of Bali, Pura Besakih, lies on the slopes of Mount Agung.

'The four of us enjoyed Balinese dancing and viewing all the exotic sights on the island. One of the unique spectacles took place one night when we witnessed a performance of a dance called the Monkey Dance, which is also known as the Kecak Dance, by an entire village of over a hundred people. Although it is now well known to tourists to Bali, it originates from the 1930s, so we would have been seeing it as a very real tribal dance and not after it became more commercialised. It is especially unique and possibly the most dramatic of all Balinese dances. Using a mixture of both dance and storytelling, the Kecak Dance depicts the Hindu epic, 'Ramayana', which tells the story of Prince Rama, who with the help of the monkey-like Vanara defeats the evil King Ravana to rescue his Princess Sita. Kecak also has roots in Sanghyang, a sacred ritual based on the idea that during the performance, hyangs, or spiritual entities, will enter and possess the bodies of the dancers. This took place in a holy temple and I can still recall how brightly the moon shone overhead and reflected against the temple walls. The villagers danced wildly almost to the point of working themselves into a trance. It did not matter to them that they were only performing to an audience of four.

I found the Balinese to be incredibly hospitable. Bali may now be filled with tourists, but when your mother and I visited in the early 1960s, it was very different and I think that we may actually have been the only tourists there at the time.

'It was in Indonesia that I first heard the dulcet tones of the singer Mahalia Jackson. I adored the sound of her voice. When I returned to Belfast, I went down to Smithfield, which no longer exists, to a record shop. I asked the owner did he have any Mahalia Jackson, to which the owner gave me a very knowing smile. "I do indeed," he said. And then he said, "Can I tell you a story about Mahalia Jackson? I had emigrated to New York and was feeling incredibly homesick. One night I was sitting in a bar, wondering what on earth I was doing so far from home. There was a radio playing in the pub and as I nursed my pint and my sorrow, the soft voice of Mahalia Jackson came on to the radio, as she sang 'The Londonderry Air'. I got up, walked out of the pub, found a travel agent and booked myself a ticket back to Belfast. It is thanks to Mahalia Jackson that I am standing here serving you today!"

'I love that story as I can just hear the soulful voice of Mahalia Jackson and picture that man sitting alone in a New York bar.

'I would probably have been offered another contract to stay in Indonesia after my first two-year stint, but country was entering a period of political unrest – as Sukarno, the President of Indonesia, felt that Malaya was going to attack Indonesia. All British citizens were told to evacuate

Indonesia, so Shirley went home to Northern Ireland on her own – she was also very keen to get home to see her own mother and sister – while I finished up my contract.

'When I was getting ready to return home, I knew it may be the last chance I would have to be in Asia for some time, so I decided to do some travelling on my way back to Ireland.

'I used to play golf in Indonesia with a friend of mine called Harry Hann, who was also a doctor. Harry had moved to Japan and invited me to visit him in Tokyo where the Olympic Games were being held in 1964. As the company had given me a first-class ticket home, I exchanged it for standard class so that I could use the extra money to visit as many places as I could on my trip back to Ireland. I started out from Indonesia and travelled via Bangkok and Hong Kong before going to Tokyo. After watching some of the Olympics, I then went on to Taiwan, the Philippines, Fiji, Tahiti, Hawaii, San Francisco and New York before flying to Dublin. I never did make my golf appointment with Harry Hann, though, because I was held up in Hong Kong by a force nine gale.

'When I eventually got to the hotel in Tokyo, it was all incredibly organised. The Olympics had started a few days before I arrived and you could buy photos from each of the day's events. The hotel also arranged transport to and from the stadium every day – it was a magnificent opportunity and an unforgettable one. I saw the 1,500 metres being won by Peter Snell from New Zealand and the 200 metres which was won by Henry Carr of the United States in a new world record time of 20.3 seconds. I also saw Maeve Kyle (no relation) running in the ladies 400 metres and I got a photograph of her.

'After leaving Japan, I headed for Taiwan as I was interested in attending an exhibition on Chinese porcelain taking place there. I always loved the uniqueness and beauty of Chinese porcelain. It was a fascinating exhibition but I didn't end up buying anything – I had however bought some in Indonesia, which I had to get shipped back to Ireland.

'After three or four days in Taiwan where I dined on their very unique-tasting Chinese food, I then went on to Manila where I was supposed to be getting an immediate connection to Australia. However, on arriving in Manila, there was a problem with the plane that, unlike the other passengers, I was delighted about as it meant I got to spend a night there and see a bit of Manila. I then went on to Sydney to visit Fred Anderson, who had been the best man at my wedding. It was great to catch up with an old friend and we had a great time reminiscing and Fred showed me some of the sights of Sydney. From Sydney, I went to Fiji, spent two or three days there and from there on to Tahiti. In Tahiti, I went for a picnic and enjoyed roast pig and swam in the crystal-blue waters around the island. It was idyllic to put it mildly. From Tahiti, I travelled to Hawaii and stayed near Waikiki Beach and enjoyed more sunshine and hospitality.

'From Hawaii, the next stop was San Francisco. I had lovely memories of my 1953 tour there and was able to meet up with some of the rugby guys I had played against on the tour. From there, I flew on to New York and then went back to Dublin.

'My only regret is that I didn't keep a diary because, although I can remember certain things, there is so much you forget with the passage of time and a diary would have recorded it all. It was a dream holiday and I returned to Ireland feeling well rested and ready for my next surgical position.'

CHAPTER NINE

A NEW LIFE
IN ZAMBIA

'The purpose of human life is to serve,
and to show compassion and the will to help others.'
Albert Schweitzer, theologian, philosopher
and medical missionary in Africa

We had reached the part of Dad's life story in which I was
able to share some of the memories – starting with his time
in Zambia. Dad and I reminisce about Zambia all the time
anyway, but there is always more to discover and I want to
know more about how he ended up there in the first place.
We settled in for a chat on a fresh spring morning and I
suggested to Dad that he go right back to the beginning of
how he got a job in Zambia.

❀

'About six months after my return to Ireland, in 1964, I began to consider the idea of going abroad again. I knew I didn't want to settle down in Ireland yet, I wasn't ready – and Shirley had enjoyed her time in Indonesia, so I thought she would probably be open to the idea of going abroad again. By chance, or perhaps by fate, depending on how you view the random circumstances of life, I noticed an advertisement in the *British Medical Journal* for a job in Zambia as a consultant surgeon, and I decided to apply.

'I knew nothing of Zambia but, as I said previously, the idea of working in a developing country appealed to me. Little did I know then that I would end up spending thirty-four and a half years of my life in Central Africa. I find it fascinating that just by the small fact of happening to see a job advertisement, I changed not only the course of my life, but of your mum's and yours and Caleb's.

'The job was situated in the small mining town of Chingola, which is on the Copperbelt of Zambia about twenty miles from the Congolese border. Following an interview process and after discussing it with Shirley, who although initially a little unsure, came around to the idea and was quite happy to have another adventure abroad, I accepted the job and we moved to Chingola in 1966.'

Zambia is a land-locked country that had gained its independence in 1964 – before then it was known as Northern Rhodesia (what is now Zimbabwe was Southern Rhodesia), though it is still a member of the

Commonwealth. It is a massive country of 290,000 square miles. Compared to other African countries, it is relatively peaceful and has never experienced any army coups or attempted military or personal dictatorships. Kenneth Kaunda was the president for most of Dad's time there, from 1964 to 1991, and was replaced in democratically held elections by President Chiluba. Zambia had a form of government called 'participatory democracy', which meant that different candidates stood for parliament, but they were all in the one party – effectively, it was a one-party state. However, this changed in 1991 when Frederick Chiluba, the head of the Movement for Multiparty Democracy, came to power.

The country's main export is copper. It is made up of about 4–5 per cent pure copper, which is a very high quality, much higher than that mined in many countries (copper is mined as copper sulphides and usually has a pure copper percentage from about 0.4–1 per cent).

There were a lot of expatriates working in Zambia as engineers in the copper mines, as well as in the legal profession, and some of the wives worked as nurses, teachers or secretaries. There was also a large Zambian population which comprised many tribes, such as the Bemba, the Tonga, the Lundi and the Ngoni. Tribalism did exist, but the Zambian people are quite a peaceful people and for the most part worked and lived within their tribes and avoided conflict.

'I found one of the advantages of living in Chingola was the climate. Chingola is 4,000 feet above sea level and has a superb climate. There are two seasons – a rainy season and a dry season. The rainy season begins at the end of October and lasts until March and then the dry season takes over and lasts from April until October. Zambia never felt cold to me, except perhaps during the evenings and early mornings in July when the temperature might drop to between eight and ten degrees Celsius and you might need to put on another layer of clothes. The beauty of the climate in Zambia is the lack of humidity, unlike many of the countries on the west coast of Africa. The only time you might experience a bit of humidity is in October, the hottest month of the year, just before the rains begin. The sun goes down every evening at six o'clock and there is little variation in this throughout the year. Enjoying the sunset was part of life in Zambia.

'I flew out to Zambia ahead of Shirley, who, again, spent more time packing up all our belongings she wanted to bring and saying her final goodbyes, so she joined me a few months later. The position I was offered was consultant surgeon in the two local hospitals, which were called North Hospital and South Hospital. The hospitals were run by the Zambia Consolidated Copper Mines and we treated not only miners and their families but everyone in the surrounding area. When I first moved to Chingola, I was the only trained surgeon in either hospital or, for

The entrance to South Hospital, Chingola, Zambia.

that matter, in the nearby town of Chililabombwe [which means 'the town of the croaking frog'] fifteen miles away.

'During colonial times, the surgeons were only there for the expatriates, who attended South Hospital – the local Zambians attended North Hospital, which was much busier.

'I was disappointed to discover that surgeries were being carried out in North Hospital by doctors who were not officially trained surgeons. One example I remember clearly is a thyroid operation. The recurrent laryngeal nerves, which control the vocal chords, had been cut, which meant that they could not move at all. Consequently, the patient couldn't breathe properly because the vocal chords came together and prevented air from entering the lungs. An emergency tracheostomy had to be done, to enable the patient to breathe.

'This never should have happened and so I arranged to start clinics right away at North Hospital, as well as surgeries. An opportunity to make a vast improvement came my way when the Chief Medical Officer went on leave. I didn't tell him about the changes I had planned because administration would have delayed the process interminably. We had a very good doctor called Dr Mahesh Travedi sitting in South Hospital, who dealt with the often minor conditions of the expatriates. I went to him and said, "Mahesh, I want you to go down to North Hospital and take over the running of the wards there, because the patients are being sorely neglected."

'He was only too delighted to be given a chance to practise some proper medicine and to have the increased responsibility. I always said if you wanted to please Mahesh, give him a new medical textbook. I was delighted to know that an excellent experienced doctor was now in charge in North Hospital. By the time the CMO came back, the change was made and there wasn't a lot he could do about it.

'Most of the surgeries took place at North Hospital and general consultations took place at South Hospital, which was conveniently located about a five-minute drive from our house. Callouts during the night were frequent. Being a surgeon, you work very irregular hours, so being able to have a quick nap became essential for me to recharge – I am very lucky that I can cat nap wherever and whenever

I need to. I usually had a quick twenty-minute snooze at lunch-time.

'Zambia had a population of about ten and a half million when I arrived in 1966. There was no medical school to produce doctors for the country, but one was set up in the late 1960s which still only produces sixty to seventy doctors a year. The issue of a lack of personnel continued throughout my whole time there. I had to deal with the reality that the country had no neurosurgeons, no vascular surgeons and no plastic surgeons, and there were no obstetricians or gynaecologists in Chingola, so I had to be prepared to turn my hand to any and every type of surgical condition. This meant that all diagnoses were clinical. For example, with a head injury, you would work on the Glasgow Coma Scale and watch patients very carefully in case there was pressure building up inside their brains, which would mean having to do a burr hole.

'A few years after I arrived in Chingola, I was joined by another surgeon called Mr Daz and, in the 1990s, I worked with a very good Zambian surgeon called Dr Mugala, who had trained in Lusaka and done a year's endoscopy training in the UK.

'The hospital did have x-ray diagnostic facilities along with a consultant radiologist and they could get enemas and barium swallows, but there were no scanning facilities and it was not until the 1980s that the hospital obtained an ultrasound machine. There was no treatment for cancer of any description – no radiotherapy, chemotherapy or any cancer drugs – so the only option for cancer patients was surgery.

'North Hospital had about 500 beds, including maternity and gynaecological wards, children's wards, male and female surgical wards and medical wards, and South Hospital had about a hundred beds. North Hospital treated the local people who worked in the copper mines and their families, but was also open to anyone. The population of Chingola was over 100,000 and the catchment area for the two hospitals meant we could be dealing with up to a quarter of a million people. I performed surgeries on many different parts of the body and also operated on newborn babies with surgical problems.'

'How did you prepare for all those surgeries, when you had no idea what you were going to be faced with?'

Dad leaned back with a sigh, remembering how he dealt with many conditions he didn't know much about. 'All you could do was to go back to the books. I mean, if you didn't do it, nobody else was going to, so you tended to get over any nerves or apprehension fairly quickly. I recall my first hysterectomy when I was a bit nervous because there was a chance of cutting the ureters, which are little tubes that carry urine from the kidney to the bladder. I had seen ureters accidentally cut in that operation before and I was determined that it was not going to happen either to me or, more importantly, my patient, so I took a lot of care during that operation.'

Surgery out in Africa brought these kinds of challenges every day and Dad was constantly reading and coming up with improved ideas for surgeries and procedures. Throughout my childhood, I recall very clearly a surgical book so big that I could hardly lift it, which would rest open on Dad's desk, usually with some grim picture of an operation or some technical description that was indecipherable to my young eyes. This was what I called my father's 'go to' book, where he would frequently be found asleep, head lying on top of the open book, late at night.

'When I first arrived in Chingola, I was put up in the company guest house before I was allocated a house, at 41 7th Street. I remember the guesthouse being very luxurious and I stayed there for three or four days before we were able to move into our home.'

Chingola has a system of streets that run from 1st to 14th, with some bigger houses located in avenues that run opposite the streets on the way into the town centre. Many of the houses in Chingola were large and spacious and the majority had swimming pools. A few years later, my parents moved to 9 Oppenheimer Avenue and this is where my brother and I grew up and where Dad remained for the rest of his time in Africa.

I adored our house in Oppenheimer Avenue. It was a large detached white bungalow, although it was decorated

Road sign for Oppenheimer Avenue.

with old furniture and wasn't what you would call opulent. It had a fantastic amount of space and was a very relaxed house, with many visitors and friends popping in. It had a large spacious area leading out to the garden with a bar for entertaining, a large, open-plan dining room and lounge and the bedrooms were huge in comparison to many houses back in Ireland. There were four large bedrooms and Dad's had an ensuite bathroom and a dressing room. We had to have netting on the windows to ensure that snakes couldn't climb through them and it also kept out the mosquitos. Outside there was a veranda complete with tables and chairs and an old-fashioned swing. Our garden was about half an acre in size and it had two levels which sloped down towards the back gate of the local golf

Our house on Oppenheimer Avenue:
from the front (above) and the back garden (below).

club. Bougainvillea and jacaranda trees adorned the front
garden, and the back garden was home to a large variety of
plants, flowers and trees including roses, frangipanis and
jacarandas as well as mango, avocado and flame trees.

'We had a lovely set-up in Chingola and it was an ideal
place to raise children. When you were young, you and

Caleb came to me and asked if you could keep a dog that our neighbour was going to give you. I was very reluctant because I knew I would be the one who ended up looking after it, but you pleaded so much that I relented.'

'Ah, you loved 2K really! He was good company for you when we were at boarding school.'

Ours was the perfect garden to have a dog. His name – 2K – stood for 'two Kwacha', which was the cost to buy the dog and was a pittance. My brother Caleb and his friend Mark had bought 2K when he was a puppy from some Zambians up in the town who sadly were not treating the dog well. Mark had him first, but as his family were due to leave the country, he was given to us. A cuter wee pup you never saw in your life. He was part Alsatian, part lots of other things (most of which we never found out!). He had a beautiful golden coat and a face similar to that of a Labrador. He was loyalty itself and was the most loving dog right from the start. Caleb and I adored him.

'When you were kids and you used to write to me from boarding school, the first line of the letter was always about him: "How's 2K?" "Are you giving him enough attention?" "Are you still getting him the good bones from the butcher?" I knew where I stood in the scheme of things!'

'And whenever you wrote back, the first thing I would do was scan the letter for 2K's name. When he was a puppy and it was time for me to go back to boarding school, I

2K, our faithful dog who was a joy to come home to.

would drag my suitcase out from under the bed. 2K used to immediately know I would be leaving and he would jump into the suitcase to try and prevent me from packing. It used to break my heart. When we came home from boarding school for the holidays, my favourite part was running out to the garden to call him. He would stop dead and stare at me for a second as if in disbelief that I was home, and then come bounding over so fast, I had to grab him to make sure he didn't knock me over.'

2K lived a good long life and died during my final year at university in 1994.

It was customary for expatriate families to employ local people to work in their houses and gardens. Dad employed two locals called Tyson and Kwema. Tyson did the cooking and cleaning and Kwema was 'in charge' of the garden, though I don't think I saw him do a day's gardening in his life. It was a family joke that whenever we had lunch outside, Kwema would come out into the garden and ensure that we saw him drag the sprinkler from one side of the garden to the other. Sometimes we would find him lying in a drug-induced haze on the lawn – he was a little too fond of the *baci baci*, as cannabis was known to the locals. He was, however, a very faithful and honest employee and was an important part of our family. He also faithfully served up breakfast for Dad (and us when we were there) for nearly thirty years and hardly ever missed a day. Kwema lived in a small house located within a large yard area at the back of our house, known as a *kaya*, which in Zulu means 'house' or 'at home'.

Tyson turned out not to be as faithful or honest as Kwema, and we discovered that he had been stealing not only money but many other items. He was replaced by a very nice man called White. Tyson and Kwema had tolerated each other and had never really been great friends, whereas White and Kwema got along fine because they were from the same tribe.

Dad continues to reminisce about the lifestyle in Chingola.

'Many of my family and friends had thought I was very foolhardy to even consider going to live in the depths of Central Africa. I imagine they envisaged wild jungle, no running water, disease and dirt. Every time they came out to visit, family would be incredulous at the life of luxury that we were living, with *braais* [the local word for a barbeque], swimming and parties the norm. Playing golf, swimming and tennis were readily available and cost almost nothing, and the day often ended with a drink at sunset, called "sundowners". They soon realised I had in fact made a very wise decision.

'There were times we did have shortages of bread or sugar or butter, but they didn't usually last long and there was always more than enough other food to make up for whatever was in short supply. A particular favourite of mine was the Nile perch, a local fish that we dined on at least once a week. There was another good local fish called the *buka buka*. I also remember luscious fruit salads, an abundance of tomatoes, avocadoes, gem squash and ice-cream! Tyson was famous for his roast chicken, which we usually had on a Saturday night. It was stuffed with breadcrumbs, fragranced with rosemary and thyme and the skin was rubbed in herbs and oil. I always remember yours and Caleb's friends would always ask, before they decided if they were going to stay over, whether Tyson was making his roast chicken, and as he usually made it on a Saturday night, it became quite a busy one in our house, usually with friends of yours or Caleb's and often both staying over. I used to say, "We may not be millionaires, but we live like them!"

'Dinner parties were a common occurrence and we

often had six or eight people round the dining room table. Tyson and Kwema, or later on, White and Kwema, would don their white chef outfits and hugely enjoyed the kudos they received for making their specialities and providing us with a delicious meal.

'Life as a surgeon in Zambia did not start gently. A few days after starting my job, a lorry loaded with Zambians accidentally hit an elephant on the Solwezi Road, which runs out of Chingola, and a lot of people were thrown off the back of the lorry and onto the road. There were a lot of injuries and multiple operations had to be performed. So it was rather a baptism of fire and not having any time to think, which was probably just as well, otherwise I may well have packed my bags and run!

'Shortly after that, in Kitwe, a town about forty kilometres from Chingola, a car crossed the level crossing at the wrong moment and was hit by a train and the wounded were brought to the hospital in Chingola. There were a lot of people injured and I had to perform many operations that night, including the removal of two ruptured spleens.

'I mostly did a lot of routine operations – and mainly ones that related to hernias. There were operations on tumours, such as tumours of the kidney and of the bowel, and with no ultrasound machines to help diagnose the condition, the only option was to operate.

'As there were few specialist surgeons, I do remember

some special operations, one of them being a man with a stab wound to the heart who had a cardiac tamponade. This is where the blood flows out of the heart and doesn't escape from the pericardium, which surrounds the heart, therefore compresses the heart and stops it beating properly. When I opened the pericardium the blood shot up into the ceiling like a fountain. Fortunately, the stab wound was in the left ventricle, so I was able to get a finger over the opening, stop the bleeding, call for a stitch and I managed to close the hole with a suture. I was greatly relieved to see the patient sitting up in bed the following day.

'A second operation that I recall well was a patient who had been in a bad accident and had a collapsed lung and several fractured ribs. Usually you would put in a chest tube, and hope that the air would be released and the lung would expand. However, with this patient, when the tube was inserted, air kept flowing out every time he took a breath which meant that a large bronchus [part of the airway to the lungs] was probably ruptured. Unfortunately when the chest was opened, I discovered that one of the main bronchia was almost torn in two; I managed to suture it and leave in the chest tube where fortunately it all held up. I was very fortunate to have a very good anaesthetist to work alongside called Hemant Mahagaonkar – he became a great friend and we often played golf together too. He wrote up that operation in a medical journal as it had been quite an unusual one.

'I also dealt with quite a few shotgun wounds. One night, an Indian gentleman was brought in to the hospital as he had been shot on the left side of his abdomen by some criminals – the bullet had gone across the inside of the abdomen and had lodged on the right side. The descending colon had a hole in it and there were also four holes in different parts of the small bowel. I remember suturing the holes in the small bowel and also in the descending colon. Knowing it was often difficult to be sure that a hole in the descending colon would remain sutured, I did a transverse colostomy, which is an opening above the wound which meant that the bowel contents did not pass over the sutured colon until it had time to heal. I thought that the patient would have a very difficult time after the operation but it was very pleasing that he recovered well and eventually the transverse colostomy was closed, the bowel returned to the abdomen and the abdominal wound closed.

'Cancer of the oesophagus was a particularly difficult condition to treat and often by the time it was diagnosed it was quite advanced and the only option open to us was to insert a tube past the narrowing which dilated the oesophagus and enabled the patient to swallow, but this was only a palliative measure. Palliation may not have offered a cure, but it was very important as it provided a relief from pain and a temporary improvement in the patient's condition.

'It was a tradition in Zambia for family and friends to visit a patient in hospital to show that there had been no witchcraft practised on the patient by any of the family and the visitors were well disposed towards the patient. This was also the reason why funerals were such large affairs with plenty of wailing and crying.

'Although not very common, I also had to operate on children with hydrocephalus, a condition where fluid accumulates in the brain. We had to ensure that the fluid had to be drained from the ventricles in the brain, otherwise the child's skull would expand and eventually the head would become grossly enlarged. This condition must be treated before the skull enlarges, so a valve or a tube is put into one of the ventricles and has to be drained, either into the heart or the abdomen. At first I had to drain the fluid from the ventricle into the jugular vein, which was very tricky, but later you could bring the tube directly from the ventricle of the brain underneath the chest wall and directly into the abdomen, which made it much simpler.

'I also had to act as both gynaecologist and obstetrician, as there were neither of these specialists in Chingola for the first few years I was there. I was fairly nervous the first time I did a caesarean section, but I also remember the joy of seeing a new life coming into the world.'

The lack of a gynaecologist impacted on my parents directly a year after they arrived in Zambia, when my mother was pregnant with Caleb. She and Dad returned to Ireland for his birth, whereas when I was due to be born in 1971, Dad was happy for Mum to have me in Chingola because by that time there was a gynaecologist.

'As well as the routine operations and the satisfaction from helping patients through surgery, there were times when things didn't go to plan.

'I recall being approached by our physician Dr Travedi about a young girl who had a constrictive pericarditis which was probably due to an infection, maybe TB, where the pericardium was constricting her heart and preventing it from beating properly. Unless this constriction was removed, eventually her heart would fail. I had never done this operation before, but I prepared very carefully

Our young family in Chingola.

for it and I read of the dangers, especially when you got to the auricles and you had to take the pericardium from the auricles, which are a very thin part of the heart compared with the ventricles. The heart was exposed and it was possible to remove the pericardium from the left ventricle – the difficult part was removing it from the auricles. I had hoped that when I removed the pericardium from higher up that the heart would beat better, but the anaesthetist told me there was no change. I had to try and remove the pericardium from the auricles. Unfortunately the pericardium was bound very tightly to the auricles and during a careful dissection a hole was made in the thin part of the heart. Before I was able to close the hole, the anaesthetist told me that the patient's heart had stopped and she died on the table. These are operations which a surgeon never forgets and remain with him or her all of their life. Of all the successful operations I did, this one that failed is the one that has never left me.'

So many people during my life have told me how much Dad helped them when they were ill, performing this operation or that operation. Many people have actually told me that if it wasn't for Dad, they wouldn't be alive. He has saved so many lives and yet it is the pain of the one that didn't work out that has stayed with him, which I find understandable but very sad.

'There were many perils to just surviving in Zambia – between malaria, bilharzia, thyroid problems and AIDS, the worst of them all, so I didn't really give much thought to the other random occurrences of life, such as car accidents, which were frequent out in Chingola with no rules of the road other than the occasional 'STOP' sign.

'I first started seeing AIDS patients in the early 1980s and like all doctors who knew nothing of the virus, I was completely baffled by this strange illness. Following official medical news of the virus, I was horrified by the number of patients presenting with its symptoms. By the late 1980s, AIDS was becoming commonplace in Zambia. It later became clear, although at the time we didn't know it, that the local gynaecologist, Dr Patel, a third-generation Indian and a very good friend of mine, had died from the disease. He may have contracted it from a needle stick injury or through blood contact. There was no treatment then and sadly he contracted tuberculosis and died. I was asked to speak at his funeral and it was a very difficult time, trying to find the right words for his family. I remember on one particular night at the hospital five patients died from AIDS. It was a tragedy unfolding before our eyes.

'AIDS was the scourge of Africa. We were caught in a terrible predicament, because if you told the patient they had the virus, the first thing they were likely to do was to go to the local witch doctor.

'Educating the local people was a big problem because they refused to listen to the dangers of sexual promiscuity, though this changed when Kenneth Kaunda's son died of

AIDS in 1986. To his great credit, the president did not deny it or try to hide what had happened, but came out and admitted it, which then made it all right for Zambians to talk about it and learn more about it.

'I was unable to help many people who contracted the full-blown virus, because there weren't many drugs available for treatment and those that there were were too expensive for most Zambians. It was a truly desperate situation.

I had also to be very careful not to contract the HIV virus, but I wouldn't say I was afraid of it, as I often used two sets of gloves when operating, covering the first set with an iodine preparation before putting on the second set.

'The statistics of people dying from AIDS in Africa are still tragic. At one stage around 60 per cent of the population suffered from the virus. There was neither the money for the antiviral drugs nor any treatment for those who had contracted the virus and so there was very little we could do for the people, which was incredibly frustrating and sad. I used to talk to the golf caddies and plead with them not to visit prostitutes or to be sexually promiscuous. Sometimes they listened, but there were far too many people who died as a result of the spread of the virus.'

'I remember, Dad, when we went back to Zambia, one of your caddies came up to me and told me how you had saved his life by sorting out his STD and now he wouldn't sleep with women anymore. I didn't know where to look!'

There were lighter moments for Dad too. Like the

woman he treated for obesity. He told her, 'I want you to eat regularly for two days, then skip a day, and then eat regularly again for two days, and so on. Do this for two weeks and the next time I see you, you should have lost at least five pounds.'

When the woman returned two weeks later, she shocked Dad because she had lost nearly twenty pounds. 'It was unbelievable,' Dad said. 'I congratulated her for following the instructions so well.'

The woman smiled and said, 'I'll tell you, though, I thought I was going to drop dead on the third day.'

'From hunger?' Dad asked.

'No, from skipping.'

'There was also the lady who came into my clinic one day to get me to sign her passport photograph to witness that it was a true likeness, but she said to me, "but could you add … it does not do her justice".

'I guess the one and only drawback of us living out in Zambia was that you and Caleb had to go to boarding school, but I remember when I suggested that I could come back to Northern Ireland, you were both nearly hysterical at the thought of having to leave Zambia.'

'I remember the conversation very well and there was no way either Caleb or I wanted to leave Zambia. We loved living there more than anything, it was fantastic, but it was quite tough initially having to go to boarding school, at least it was for me, I can't speak for Caleb.'

'One of the benefits of my job was that ZCCM [Zambia Consolidated Copper Mines, the company that Dad worked for], agreed to send children abroad to a boarding school of the parents' choice and ZCCM paid for their fares and boarding fees. I always felt it was extremely important that you both received a good education, and I was delighted that you were going to have the opportunity to be educated in Northern Ireland.'

Caleb was duly sent to boarding school at Cabin Hill and then Campbell College at the age of eleven. As I had started reading Enid Blyton books on Malory Towers and St Clare's, I begged Dad to allow me to go at the same time – but I was only seven and far too young. Dad waited until I was nine before sending me to Rockport Preparatory School in County Down, I then went on to Victoria College in Belfast to do my O'levels and I completed my schooling at Methodist College Belfast where I sat my A'levels.

Had I known that the reality of boarding school was nothing at all like the books I was reading, I would have never showed such enthusiasm. I found the first couple of years difficult, but like all tough situations, it can make you stronger if you are not defeated by it. I finally settled down and have some very happy memories of my final years at boarding school.

I can still vividly see the image of Dad in his safari suit, which he always wore with a different, very stylish cravat, standing on the tarmac of the airfield, either waving us hello or goodbye. I hated the goodbyes.

My memories of living in Chingola are extraordinarily happy ones. It was a life of outdoor sports like swimming, golf and tennis mixed with parties and a lot of socialising. We had a huge number of friends, as everyone mingled because the town was so small, and I remember as a teenager my father spending a lot of his time driving us and picking us up from parties, not only in Chingola, but in the nearby town of Kitwe, where, as teenagers, we would get together to enjoy bigger parties.

Dad was our primary carer in Zambia and as a father he had a profound influence on our lives. He taught us values – having good manners, and being kind and respectful. He taught us that when you have a choice between being mean or dishonest or whatever, for whatever reason, you may go ahead and act badly, but you better be ready to pay the consequences. As children, we were not always ready to listen to his philosophical or moral arguments, but they were gently and repeatedly ingrained in us and I know they have greatly contributed to the people we are today.

Caleb and I would always talk about the 'Dad lecture'! If you had done something wrong, Dad wouldn't shout or yell, he would calmly discuss our misdemeanour and in a very quiet, calm voice tell us how disappointed he was in our behaviour. As Caleb said, this was always much more frightening that being yelled at, and as soon as he started his lecture, you could feel your lower lip start to wobble and your eyes fill with tears. Very effective, Dad! Fortunately, I don't remember too many of these occasions and I think when you are given trust you either do your best to honour it, or you make sure you don't get caught!

Living in Zambia also brought its social issues. Alcohol was cheap and cannabis was easy to obtain. Sadly some young people went completely off the rails and there were some tragedies involving young people in car and motorbike accidents. I think Dad was well aware of what was going on and used to outline the stark reality of what taking drugs and drinking too much did to your brain. This was enough to dissuade us from the drugs and although we had our moments with drink, as most young people do, luckily Caleb and I both emerged unscathed. Dad remembers other perils of life in Africa.

'I remember when you contracted malaria when you were sixteen. We were so sure you couldn't have malaria, as you hadn't been outside of the town.'

'I will never forget it. You were convinced that I must have food poisoning, as the range of the malaria mosquito was about three miles and if the authorities had sprayed the disinfectant that killed the mosquitoes just outside the three-mile area, it was believed that no malaria mosquitoes would be in the town. I remember you decided to get a blood slide done, just as a precaution, to check for the disease. We

were both pretty surprised when it came back positive. I was in bed with a high fever and constant vomiting for the first forty-eight hours. I also point blank refused to go into hospital as I was terrified of them back then and was very squeamish about needles going into my veins. I remember when you brought Dr Travedi out to see me and he agreed that if I could keep down the anti-malaria tablets, I could stay at home. Well, talk about mind over matter. Those tablets were not coming up, despite their best efforts. I forced them to stay down and so began my slow recovery. I was as weak as a kitten for about three weeks and then a good dose of sunshine and plenty of rest saw me back to full health. It made me a little more respectful of those mosquitos and from then on I always took anti-malaria tablets – though you never took them, did you?'

'No, if I thought there was a possibility I had contracted malaria, I went straight to the laboratory at the hospital and asked them to do a slide to check. It wasn't safe to take anti-malaria drugs every day because they negatively affect the liver.

'One of the other main problems we faced at the hospital was the curse of the witch doctor. More often than not, if the Zambian patient didn't like their diagnosis, or did not want to have an operation, they would run off to the witch doctor. The next time they came in to see me, the problem may have become so severe it was either inoperable or it was too late for treatment. It was impossible to hold a patient against their will and I would do all I could to try and persuade them not to visit the witch doctor, but it was a part of their culture we had to accept and could do nothing about. The Zambian people in a way found it hard to accept natural death or illness, there was always this shadow of the possibility they had been cursed hanging over them.

'There were also so many bizarre things that used to occur in Zambia, it made me quite unshockable really! One such story related to the butcher in the town, where I would sometimes buy our meat. One day the butcher's young apprentice was feeding meat into the mincer; unfortunately his hand was caught by the revolving machine and became completely mangled in the machine. Tragically when he was brought into the hospital, I had no choice but to amputate just above the elbow, as there was absolutely no way to save his arm. The apprentice was still recovering in hospital the next time I called up to the butcher. As I was leaving the shop, the butcher himself came running out to the car. I naturally assumed that he was dashing out to enquire as to the health of his poor assistant. To my utter amazement, he said, "Dr Kyle, when am I going to get my mincing machine back? All my customers are complaining because I can't give them their mince!"

'There was also the remarkable situation of a blind lady who was in her village and went out to chop some wood while she was carrying her baby. She accidentally drove the axe into the back of her baby's head. She brought the baby to the hospital and I was able to operate, by removing some the bone from the brain and suturing the coverings over the brain. The baby made a full recovery, it was miraculous. Wood had to be chopped it seemed, blind or not.

'Another aspect of living in Zambia I loved were the unique sounds and smells. I loved the sounds of the crickets and the cicadas at night. And the cockerel crowing every morning at dawn. One of my favourite sounds was on a Sunday afternoon if I sat in the garden, I could hear the sound of African drums being played. For me, Zambia had the most evocative sounds and smells of any country I have ever been in and without a doubt the most beautiful sunsets and sunrises. Getting up at five a.m. has never been as enjoyable as when you see the sun rising majestically over the horizon.'

'I couldn't agree more. It is something you have to experience, but it gets into your system and never leaves you. Mind you, I could have done without that neighbour's cockerel waking me up every morning at 5 a.m.!'

Wildlife is another interesting aspect of life in Zambia. Once you have seen animals in their native habitat, it sort of spoils you for trips to the zoo. There were however many dangers of living in Zambia, not least the snakes. I have a terrible fear of snakes to this day. We had several in our garden over the years. The most dangerous are the spitting cobra and the black mamba, which could kill you with one bite. Dad told me how my mum came out to sunbathe one day and found the twenty-foot skin of a snake lying at the back door. I also remember our dog 2K barking one day and when I came into the garden to see what he was barking at, he was standing about five feet away from a cobra who looked pretty venomous. I screamed my head off for him to come to me which he eventually did and after dragging him inside, I told Kwema, who killed the snake with little fuss, while I watched terrified in case he was attacked. He seemed completely calm though and appeared to know exactly what he was doing. It wasn't a big snake, but it was enough to frighten me for life. As for our beloved dog, he was lucky not to lose his eyesight or worse.

'*Do you remember the monkeys too? They used to drive me nuts on the golf course when they would jump down from the trees and steal the golf balls.*'

'They could be pretty irritating all right, but you got used to them. I remember when we were on holiday in Kenya when you were only about seven. You used to hate the monkeys who would be roaming freely around the hotel grounds where we were staying. Crocodiles were another major hazard and not to be messed with. They are the sneakiest of creatures and thinking you are safe standing ankle deep in water can be the biggest mistake you make. One of the saddest situations I ever had to deal with related to a crocodile.

'One day as I was just about to start a clinic, a Scottish man came into my room with his wife. She was completely hysterical and in a dreadful state. Her husband quickly explained that she had been out with friends at a camp on the Kafue River over the weekend and when he and the others had left to go back on the Sunday evening, she'd decided to stay on with her two young boys for another day. The following morning she was sitting on the bank of the river and the two little boys were paddling, not even up to their knees, in the river in front of her. There was a sudden splash as a crocodile grabbed one of the little boys. I had to admit the wife to hospital for sedation, while her husband went back to the river to try and recover any parts of his son's body that the crocodile may have left.'

'That is such a tragic story. I can hardly bear to think about how traumatic it must have been for that poor family.'

'Another sad incident involving crocodiles was when the chief lab technician at South Hospital was snorkelling in one of the lakes, I think it was Lake Tanganyika. His wife and children were on the shore; sadly a crocodile grabbed hold of the man as he was snorkelling. The Chief Medical Officer at the hospital called me in and told me about this accident, he was flying up to the lake to see if there was any chance of recovering the body. He and some other men hired a plane and circled the lake. After some time, they saw the crocodile crossing the lake with the body in its mouth. They got into a speedboat and buzzed round the crocodile to try and frighten it into letting go of the body, which it eventually did, so they were at least able to recover the body for the family to lay to rest. Though it could go the other way too. I was once over visiting a friend, Mike Fisher, on his farm in Kitwe. The house overlooked a river. The previous week, a crocodile had come up on the banks of the river and taken a little dog. We were upstairs in a room overlooking the river, when the croc appeared probably hoping to find more "food". Mike quickly grabbed his gun, ran down to the river and aiming at the right spot on the crocodile's brain (because it would be useless to hit him in any other part), hit him exactly on target, the crocodile spun round a few times at a dizzying speed and then floated down the river. It was quite a spectacle.

'The other animal in Zambia you had to respect is the hippo, which is considered to be the most dangerous animal in Africa. One of my colleagues at South Hospital back in the 1970s went out to a lake with some friends. His boat was upturned by a hippo and the three men on-board were flung into the air and according to the two men who survived, the unlucky man came down right into the jaws of the hippo. In Zambia, you best respect the wildlife.'

Sometimes Caleb or I would be invited to go to a place

called Kariba Dam, or to other dams nearer to Chingola. Kariba Dam is one of the largest dams in the world, standing 128 metres (420 feet) tall and 579 metres (1,900 feet) long. Families would take their speedboats out, if they were lucky enough to have one. The men would fish during the day and we would have *braais* at night and all sit around a campfire. It was heaven for us when we were young. Dad never liked us going on these trips but, to his credit, he allowed us to go. However, every single time we were heading off, we were warned in no uncertain terms that if he heard that we had so much as dipped our toes into the water, we would never be allowed to go again. This was not only because of the risk of crocodiles, but also of bilharzia, a parasitic disease that can be fatal. It is caused by several species of parasites, such as trematodes, a horrible worm-like creature that can cause irreparable damage if it gets under your skin. Many of the children did swim in the dam believing it to be safe, but I had been frightened enough by Dad's dire warnings that I didn't dare risk it and I am very glad now that I listened to him.

'One of my favourite memories of Zambia is the trip we took together to Luangwa Valley in 1996, which coincided with my seventieth birthday. You had a friend from university called Kam who came out on holiday and we felt we could both celebrate my birthday and take Kam to see what a good safari was all about. You had a huge amount of luggage and when I asked you what on

*With Justine on the trip to Luangwa Valley, a magnificent game park in
Zambia of about 5,000 square miles, for my seventieth birthday.*

earth you were bringing, you mumbled something about
a girl and her shoes. Of course, I later found out that it
was a suitcase full of cards and presents from the extended
family. We have that lovely photo of us sitting outside my
chalet on the morning of my birthday, just a few hundred
yards from where hippos were bathing in the Zambezi
and elephants were grazing on the bank on the opposite
side of the river. I remember being so delighted to be in
such a beautiful place for my birthday and we followed
that with a safari drive where we marvelled at the beauty
of the African wilderness, seeing lion cubs, baby zebra
and magnificent elephants in their natural environment.
It was the trip of a lifetime and one I always remember
with such affection.'

As a family, we had many other great holidays in

Zambia too. One of the trips we used to take was to the Victoria Falls. The falls flow into the River Zambezi, near the Zambia–Zimbabwe border in Livingstone. When I was young, Dad drove Caleb and me there a few times, and we would always stop for a picnic en route. It was a long drive, about ten hours, so we would set off early in the morning and arrive in time for a late dinner. We always stayed at the Musi-O-Tunya Intercontinental Hotel in those days because, as residents, we could pay for it in Kwacha, which was the local currency and actually had some value back in the 1970s, until inflation began to go berserk in the 1980s and it devalued rapidly. The hotel was fairly plush with delicious food. The falls themselves were majestic, they are about 5,000 feet wide and 300 feet high. As we arrived, we could hear what the locals call the *musi-o-tunya* which means 'the smoke that thunders' in reference to the incredible roar of the water gushing over the falls. The mist coming from them can be seen up to twelve miles away. It was spectacular. Even though we went there probably about half a dozen times, they were magnificent each and every time we saw them.

'I used to love those trips to the Victoria Falls. It also reminds me of your fascination with David Livingstone. Whenever we brought a friend out to Zambia for a holiday, you would give your Livingstone and Stanley talk, and although as a teenager I rolled my eyes heavenward at the thought of hearing it again, I can obviously now appreciate what a good

story it makes and how interesting it was for anyone visiting the Victoria Falls. I never knew what triggered your interest in the subject though.'

'Well, if I become interested in a subject, I can become thoroughly engrossed in learning as much as I can about it – and such was the case with the life of David Livingstone. The first book I read on the subject was *Livingstone's Last Journey* by Reginald Copeland, which is about what took place after Stanley had found Livingstone and Livingstone had decided not to return to England because he was still searching for the source of the Nile. Unfortunately Livingstone was going in completely the wrong direction and actually headed towards the Congo, which started from two lakes in Zambia, so he ended up in Zambia and that is where he died in the early 1870s.

'However, my interest really began before that. The matron of the hospital in Chingola once asked me to deliver some towels to a hospital I was going to visit up the Great North Road. The hospital in Chingola could no longer use them because they dated from before the time that Zambia received its independence and they were labelled with the words "European Hospital" or "African Hospital", and this was no longer acceptable to be seen on towels. Although apartheid did not exist officially in Zambia, there were still places where Zambians were not allowed to enter, such as certain clubs which were only open to the expatriates. This process was to change over time with a process known as "Zambianisation" where the expatriates would train the Zambians, who would then be placed in their jobs.

'So I took these towels up to a hospital there, which was run by a doctor called Milton Curry, a quiet man who experienced great tragedy in his life when he had to operate on his own wife, who tragically died.

'Milton asked me if I would like to go out to the clinic of the hospital near Chitambo, a village in southern Zambia. The ambulance was going out there to pick up a man who had what was known as sleeping sickness, caused by the bite of a tsetse fly. He told me that the memorial to Livingstone was near to the clinic, and, if I liked, the ambulance could take me to see the spot where Livingstone died. I was intrigued and loved the idea and was kindly taken there by the ambulance driver. It is a very stark memorial with nothing but a stone cross with the date of Livingstone's death engraved upon it. That was what really sparked my interest, I suppose. When I retired and had a bit more time, I continued to read a huge amount on the subject of Stanley and Livingstone and indeed I have been invited to speak on the topic, which I thoroughly enjoyed.'

'*What was it like for you living in Chingola back then? It was such a tight-knit community, was it easy to adjust to life there?*'

'Chingola was a small town, so there was always a bit of gossip and everybody knew your business. I always felt a bit like the local psychiatrist as well as surgeon, as I always had a never-ending queue of people lining up to tell me their problems.'

'That is because you are such a good listener and you can listen without judging people. I think you have a special empathy.'

'Well, I would say more that it was my role as a doctor which meant it was my duty to listen to those in trouble without judging them. I do find people's stories fascinating though. Everyone, no matter who they are, has a story to tell.'

'I have such vivid memories of people calling to the house at all hours of the day and night and you sitting with them up at the bar while they poured out their troubles.'

'Well, we also had a lot of friends who called in for a drink and that was very different, just a social occasion.

'One of the more difficult aspects of being a doctor was trying to comfort those who had lost a loved one. Sadly I had to comfort several different families at different times who had lost someone to suicide. I knew a young man in Chingola who committed suicide and I was a good friend of the family. They asked me to speak at the funeral. The parents were in a terrible state, feeling that they should or could have done something to prevent what had happened. All I could say was that it was not for those left behind to blame themselves and if they looked to religion or history they would see that even Jesus could not stop Judas from taking his own life. It is of course understandable that you could never come to terms with someone taking their own life and that is why I feel so strongly about there being as many resources and as much help and support as possible available to people who need it.

'Whilst we can never understand the complexity of someone who is suicidal, I wish that if people who were feeling despair could somehow reach out to someone to be reminded that, as the poem goes, "This hour is not my all of time." If they could somehow get help to understand that the "dark night of the soul" will pass and if they could only reach out to somebody, anybody, before doing something that may have tragic consequences. I appreciate that it is a hugely complex subject and one on which I am certainly not qualified to speak. I suppose being a doctor you become used to listening to people's problems, but as I hold such value on life, I wish more could be done for those feeling suicidal, as it is always such a tragedy.'

I often felt in Zambia people really took advantage of Dad's kindness on occasion. The phone never seemed to stop ringing in our house. I can honestly say that in my whole life, I never saw Dad turn away anyone in need. He's always demonstrated extraordinary kindness and compassion. Every lunch-time you would find either a Zambian standing at the door wanting medication, or someone trying to sell Dad a wooden carving or some malachite. He would tell them they had to stop coming to the door, but they just kept turning up, knowing that he would help them.

One of the parts of his job that Dad really enjoyed was his work with the Flying Doctor Service. I have never heard any details of the work he did, so I am eager to find out more.

'Dr Hemant Mahagaonkar, the anaesthetist, and I often took part in outings with Mission Medicare. This organisation, commonly known as the Flying Doctor Service, was set up to cater for the rural hospitals that had no doctors or surgeons and were often run by nurses. These rural hospitals had some basic equipment, but were lacking in personnel. I would set off sometimes with one or two other doctors on a Saturday morning. We would operate on Saturday afternoon and then we would be put up at the hospital overnight. On the Sunday we would operate in the morning and then leave in the afternoon. We went to various rural locations such as Kalini Hill, near the Benguera Swamps, which was in the northern part of Zambia bordering Tanzania.

'As the regions were so remote, the landing strips had often been prepared by local people. Flying in, I would be looking down on giraffe and elephant and buffalo. I always loved watching the local children running alongside the plane when it landed, cheering and clapping.

'On one of these trips, I was taken to see the source

of the River Zambezi. This was a great thrill for me, as having read about the geography of the area, I was very interested to see it. The plane was owned by Mission Medicare and was flown by a friend of mine called Larry Franklin. He would stay at the hospital overnight as well and being an engineer, he usually made himself busy by fixing any equipment at the hospital that had broken down. He was a very useful man and was welcomed as much as the doctors, especially if there was something to be fixed, like the television, which was their main source of entertainment in this remote area.

'Operations at Mission Medicare were varied, and I did all kinds of operations from prostates to delivering babies, to more serious operations. Whatever was required, we had to do it. On other occasions, the pilot was a man named Wolf Schmidt. He was well known around Chingola and one of his peculiarities was that he had this enormous bunch of keys hanging from his belt at all times. One Sunday when Wolf, his wife and I were returning to Chingola in a one-engine plane, he decided that he wanted to stop off at a place called Hippo to pick up something, I can't recall what it was now. This turned out to be a reckless decision, as by the time we arrived in Chingola it was dark. There were no lights at the airport, so Wolf was unable to see where the runway was and he had to keep circling the plane. I don't mind admitting I was afraid and I asked him to go back to Ndola, where there was a large airport, but Wolf was determined to try and land the plane, much to my ever-growing concern.

'Luckily for us, a very astute pilot from Chingola, Taffy Hughes, who ran the local airline, was having a party that night and all the guests were outside. He heard the plane and then noticed it continually circling overhead and knew there was a problem. With some quick thinking, he asked the guests to all drive up to the Flying Club, a few miles away, and to park in a row and point their headlights towards the landing strip, so Wolf could land the plane.

I was a very relieved man when I got off the plane and the first thing I saw was the furious face of Taffy Hughes. Taffy was livid with Wolf. Taffy kindly invited me back to his party and gave me a stiff brandy.'

Another very enjoyable aspect of life in Zambia was the theatre, in which Dad played a large part. A friend in Chingola called Paula Finlay, who was the local dentist's wife, came to Dad and asked him if he would act in *A Christmas Carol*. Dad was delighted and readily agreed, only to find that his role was to play the 'Second Portly Gent'. Dad's visions of stardom quickly vanished. He did, however, act in numerous plays after that, including playing the old man in *Noises Off*. Later he produced and acted in *The Letters of Mrs Patrick Campbell and George Bernard Shaw*, along with a friend, Mrs Raymen, who also loved the theatre.

'My great Irish friend Bob Rooney and I used to

discuss Irish literature at length and we decided to put on something Irish as a fitting farewell to Bob when he and Maisie were leaving Zambia. We wrote and produced *An Evening with Oscar Wilde*. I loved doing this and we both acted in it. I can't speak from experience to say whether it was any good or not, but other people have said it was a very enjoyable evening.'

I smile and point out to Dad his tea cup, which has printed around the top a quotation of Oscar Wilde's: 'Only dull people are brilliant at breakfast.'

Dad smiles and, after a few more of his favourite Oscar quotations, says, 'For observational humour and dry wit, he is the best, in my opinion.

'Every year at the theatre in Zambia, they invited an adjudicator to come out from the UK and judge a number of plays that would be staged as part of a theatre festival. Various towns in the Copperbelt took part, and

At the grave of Oscar Wilde in Père Lachaise Cemetery, Paris.

our little town did very well during these visits, with the theatre group winning on a number of occasions, including one play entitled *A Bequest to the Nation* by Terence Rattigan.

'In later years, the Zambian community took over the theatre. They asked me if I would go along and listen to the rehearsals and give my critique, which I was delighted to do. I was humbled when they presented me with some lovely wine glasses when I was leaving Chingola.

'I was very fortunate in Zambia to make some lifelong friends, one of whom was the minister, broadcaster, writer and former head of BBC Northern Ireland, Colin Morris. Colin studied at Oxford University and was a brilliant student.

'When I arrived in Zambia in January 1966, Colin was

With Colin Morris, Chingola, 1968.

the minister of the United Church in Chingola and head of the United Church of Zambia, which was a combination of the Methodist and Presbyterian religions. Colin was also one of the two expatriates – Stewart Gore Brown, who I will tell you more about later, was the other – who backed Kenneth Kaunda when Zambia was seeking its independence.

'Not knowing what to expect from a minister, I was delighted to find that Colin was a man with a great sense of humour and a great intellect. We formed a very strong friendship which has remained strong to this day. Every Thursday night, Colin would dine with Shirley and me and Tyson would cook a weekly Ulster fry with all the works – bacon, eggs, beans, sausages and fried bread. After dinner, we would all sit down together and watch *The High Chaparral*, which was our weekly dose of escapism!

'Colin had a certain presence when you were in his company. In fact, he became something of a guru to me because of his incredible gift of self-expression and his remarkable ability to give lectures without using any notes. I used to tell people to go to the church where Colin spoke, so that they could hear oratory the like of which they were never likely to hear again. Colin became very good friends with the president, Kenneth Kaunda, and indeed wrote several books, either about him or in conjunction with him, such as *Letters to my Children* and *Black Government*. Such was the friendship between the two that on occasion Colin and friends helped to hide Kaunda when the police were looking for him, before Zambia gained her independence in 1964.

'Colin Morris had the foresight to see that independence was coming to many of the African countries and that Kaunda and others were fighting for this. So Colin began to talk about this during his weekly sermons; that Macmillan's "wind of change" was blowing through Africa and it was time that people realised it. He stated that the Zambians would take over the country and run it. Needless to say, the expatriate community did not want to hear this and preferred to remain in blissful ignorance.

'Peggy Lawton, a good friend of Colin's, who played the organ at the church where he was minister, told me that after the service, when Colin had spoken about this, people would shake hands with him but would let him know in no uncertain terms they would not be returning to the church. In effect, his congregation deserted him within a matter of months and he was left with the few open-minded individuals who were happy to still hear his wise words. This all took place before I arrived in Zambia in 1966.

'Ian Smith in Zimbabwe was the same – he could not believe the day would come when he would no longer govern the country and there would not be an expatriate government. He was unable to release the mantle of power and we know how that ended; hundreds of people were killed as a result, when war broke out between the local Zimbabwean people, who were seeking to take over, and the expatriates, who wanted to retain power. I knew several people who were affected by that war in Zimbabwe. Sheila Heiliason, the secretary at South Hospital, lost her son in that war and I had to remove a bullet from Bryn Hughes' back. Bryn was the son of the aforementioned Taffy Hughes, the local pilot in Chingola.

'One of the reasons I believe we did not experience more antagonism from the Zambian population was due to men such as Colin Morris and Sir Stewart Gore Brown, who were ambassadors of change and showed support to the Zambian people and who backed Kaunda. Kaunda therefore became well disposed towards the expatriate community.

'Personally I felt that Colin Morris deserved to be knighted for his work in Africa, but as he said, "You don't get any honours for dismantling the British Empire and handing over the country to be run by the local population!"

'I met Kaunda once. In fact, it was through Colin. One night, Colin arrived up at my door and asked me to sign a document which would make me a director of Veritas Corporation, a local publishing company. Naturally I was intrigued and delighted to be made a director of this company, as I told Colin I had never been a director of anything before. Colin dryly replied that I was not to get too excited, that it involved no money and was simply a requirement of the company to have two listed directors, but there were no responsibilities involved.

'The other director was to be Henry Oosthuizen, who, along with his wife Margo, was a great friend of mine. They were great friends for over twenty years and I was very sad when Margo died a few years ago, then Henry died not long after her. Henry and Margo were two of the most sincere, kind people I ever had the pleasure of knowing, and were true lifelong friends. I always loved it when they came to dinner, they were great fun and always full of stories and news. Henry would always keep his good wines to share with me!

'Anyway, Colin arrived up at the house one day and told me that Kaunda had said he would like to meet the two directors of Veritas Corporation. So Colin took Henry and me to Kitwe to one of Kaunda's residences and we spent over three hours with Kaunda. The president happily poured the tea and served us biscuits and sandwiches and we sat and discussed the current affairs of the day and material that he and Colin were writing. I don't really remember everything that was said, but something Kaunda said always stayed in my memory. He said that if Zambia had to be colonised he was glad it had been by the British rather than anyone else. He was quite a supporter of Queen Elizabeth II and felt the British had at least tried to look after their countries and had left a better legacy, than some other nations who had taken countries in Africa and had left them in a terrible state. I found him to be an intelligent, humble and very interesting individual. He invited us to stay to dinner, but knowing that that would have been an imposition too far, we made our excuses and said goodbye.

'Zambia was lucky to have had a president who was not power crazy and who ensured that there was a level of understanding between the Zambians and the expatriates, and I think he had the respect of both. He was also very magnanimous in his defeat in the elections in 1991. He ensured there was a peaceful transition. When you compare this to the likes of Idi Amin, Mobutu Sese Seko and Robert Mugabe, who were and are complete dictators, it is even clearer to see how important Kenneth Kaunda was to Zambia.

'I made so many good friends in Zambia, some of whom I am still in contact with. I am afraid there isn't the space or time to mention them all here, but I appreciate all the friends I had in Chingola, as well as all of the doctors and nurses I had the privilege to work alongside during my thirty odd years there. We were very lucky to meet people from so many different places, we had friends from all over the UK and Ireland as well as from South Africa and further afield. We also had a great social life in Zambia. We were spoilt for choice with the rugby club, tennis and squash club, the bowling club, the golf club, the flying club and the gymkhana club. During our last few Christmases in Zambia, the golf club would put on a luncheon for about fifty families or so and we had a raucous old time. We were all very happy to be together, parents not having seen children or visa-versa for some four months. Christmas in the sun seemed perfectly normal to us all, as it was all we knew, and I can tell you, it took me a few years to adapt to the traditional Christmas in Ireland. Do you remember the time, Justine, when you nearly didn't make it out to Zambia for Christmas?'

'I do indeed.'

In 1990 we ran into a problem one Christmas after my first term at Stirling University. It was the last time that I was going to benefit from a free flight courtesy of ZCCM. However, the Spanish exams at Stirling were always the last to take place. My final exam was not until 23 December and the next available flight to Lusaka was on the 24th. As I would be arriving in Lusaka on Christmas Day, Dad, being the wise man that he is, was very sceptical that the local flight from Lusaka to Ndola would fly as scheduled. He went to Taffy Hughes and asked if he could charter a small private plane to come and collect me in Lusaka. Dad was taking no chances. I have no idea how much this cost, but clearly, although expensive, it was nothing to what it would cost you elsewhere. In the end, Dad was helped out by another family whose daughter was also on my flight and so we both caught the connection in our own private plane! We arrived at 12.30 in Chingola, just in time to go to the golf club for Christmas lunch. As it turned out, Dad had been absolutely correct – in that the Lusaka to Ndola flight was cancelled at the last minute. So if he had not organised that plane, I would have been stuck in Lusaka airport on Christmas Day, and take it from me, it's not a place you want to spend an hour in, never mind a day.

'So when it came time to leave Zambia, did you feel ready?'

'Ah, yes. Although I left Chingola with a heavy heart after thirty-four and a half years in the town, I felt it was the right time to go home. For the whole time I worked in Zambia, I was on a contract which was renewed every three years. I felt that at the age of seventy-four it was time to leave, but I think the company may well have offered me another three-year contract and I had to think carefully about whether or not to accept.'

'Yes, there was a running joke between Caleb and me from about the mid-1990s that every time your contract was due for renewal you would say you were going to come back to Ireland, only to change your mind at the last minute and sign up for another three years. We always knew you were going to stay, so we never took you seriously. When you finally did come home in 2000, we knew you were definitely ready to come back.'

'For my work in Africa, I was awarded a Lifetime Achievement Award by the *Irish Journal of Medical*

Science and the Royal Academy of Medicine in Ireland. I am delighted they recognised the valuable work I did in Zambia, it meant a lot to me.'

In 2009, BBC Northern Ireland approached Dad to see if he would take part in *Season Ticket*, a half-hour sports programme that focused on a different aspect in the life of a well-known sportsman or woman. Having been a surgeon in Zambia for so long, as well as a rugby player, they felt Dad was a good fit for the programme and they asked him if he would be willing to go back to Zambia as part of the programme, to which he readily agreed. I was asked to go as well, a complete thrill for me, as I hadn't been back to Zambia since the late 1990s. I agreed without hesitation.

'It was great to be asked. We travelled out from London on British Airways with Roger Anderson [the producer], Thomas Kane [the presenter] and Gary McCutcheon [the cameraman]. After the initial introductions, we were soon

Chingola town centre, 2005.

bonding over lunch in Heathrow Airport. Although I had returned to Zambia in 2005, this was still a great opportunity for me to catch up with old friends and revisit some good memories. Many of our close friends had long since left Chingola, but there were about thirty or so who remained.

'You had arranged with your friend Doreen Hodgkinson to organise a short get-together on the second day of our trip. I was delighted to be back in Chingola and as we went in February, it was great to escape the winter too and enjoy a few days of sunshine.'

We stayed in a new hotel that had recently been built called the Protea Hotel, run by a lady called Alison Harte, who used to be a school teacher in Chingola. It was good to see a new hotel in Chingola, as the last time I was there, there was only one hotel and it certainly wasn't the sort of establishment to be seen in, never mind to stay in. After a flight lasting just under nine and a half hours, we battled our way through the chaos of collecting our luggage and clearing customs in Lusaka, a trial that can drain the most resilient traveller. We then had another flight in a small twelve-seater plane which took us from Lusaka to Ndola. When we arrived, we were met by a driver organised by the BBC to ferry us around for the few days of our stay.

'My first reminder of the country was the sensation of beautiful warm sunshine and no humidity. I was so delighted to be back in Zambia but I was surprised how shocked you were by the state of the roads. It is true they had denigrated a lot since I was last there, so I guess for you they must have seemed a lot worse. The potholes were so bad, that Roger called them "two-day potholes" because it would take you two days to get out of them if you got stuck in one. Every mile or so there were huge billboards advertising different mobile networks, and I remember it seemed ridiculous in the midst of miles of nothing but green bush, dirt tracks and bad roads to see these huge billboards everywhere.'

After checking into the hotel and having some lunch, Roger was keen to crack on with recording the programme, as we had a lot to do in the three days we were there. Our first stop was back to South Hospital.

'I was so warmly welcomed back by the theatre staff and Dr Mugala, the surgeon who had taken over from me. I found it a very happy experience to go back to the place where I had spent so much of my career. I loved my job and it was a huge part of my life, which had given me a sense of fulfilment, purpose and deep satisfaction. We went into the operating theatre where I had performed so many of my surgeries and where you were born!

'We then took a trip back to our old house at 9 Oppenheimer Avenue. I was prepared for it being very different, as I had seen it during my 2005 visit, but I know it would have been very different to how you remembered it.'

'You are right. I felt a strange disconnection from it. I was

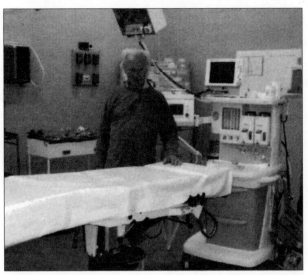

Visiting the operating theatre in South Hospital where I worked for many years, 2005.

looking at someone else's house now. It had retained none of the memories I had. They were stored in very different images. The house now had burglar bars on the windows and it seemed so different and the garden was unrecognisable. Clearly, this family had employed a proper gardener. I was unable to reconcile what I was looking at to the memories I had, they were just too different.'

The following morning we went to Chimfunshi, a chimpanzee sanctuary run by a very dedicated lady called Sheila Sydell, whom we have known for many years. The road up to the sanctuary was in a dreadful state and following a lot of rain, we had some hairy moments slowly driving over a very narrow wooden bridge with a river running rapidly below.

'I think in hindsight, it's a trip we could have done without, only in that travelling there and back took us about five hours. It was lovely to see Sheila again, though. She does incredible work looking after orphaned chimpanzees and they enjoy life in the huge sanctuary that she has built for them. We got to see some of the chimps in their enclosure and Thomas interviewed me alongside some of my chimpanzee chums, whom I knew because I had amputated an infected finger of one of the chimps over ten years earlier and there she was, still going strong!'

'Doreen, the chimp! I remember, Dad, when you were featured on a programme John Craven presented about Chimfunshi, back in the 1990s, because you got calls asking if you could help with animals if there wasn't a vet available!'

'Well, operating on a chimpanzee's finger wasn't much different to operating on a human finger!'

When we returned from Chimfunshi, we had the little tea party at the hotel that I had organised for Dad to reconnect with some good friends.

'Our very good friends George and Marena Cuturi were there. I have known them for many years and of course you grew up with their children Francois and Michelle. They invited us for dinner the following night, which was one of the highlights of the trip – good food, good wine and good company. The Cuturis had done very well in various business ventures in Chingola and they live in an incredible house set in the grounds of a stunning garden with a swimming pool.'

On our final morning in Chingola, we took the BBC crew to visit Dad's friend Samuel Bwalya, a talented Zambian artist who paints mostly wildlife, as well as a few portraits.

'Samuel is a lifelong supporter and friend of mine. He was delighted to see me and after nearly squeezing all the air out of me, he finally released me from the bear hug and took us into his house. We admired many of his paintings and he had clippings about me and a portrait he had done of me up on the wall of his house. It was a pleasure to see him again and I was reminded of how easy it is to bring joy to someone with just a quick visit.

'It was wonderful to go back. I accept that things must change and knew that inevitably Chingola would have changed. But I could still enjoy the memories I had there and the trip was more about seeing old friends again for me.'

'My experience was slightly different. Everything I associated with Chingola had gone. My friends had all gone, as had most of the families I had known. The golf club was the only place that seemed to have retained some of its elegance, and visiting it brought back many happy memories of playing golf there with you and other friends.'

Dad took the trip in his stride and, despite his health not being 100 per cent, he was as ever like Peter Pan, full of energy and enjoying every moment of it. The BBC did a good job with the documentary and it will be nostalgic in years to come to look back on it and realise once again how blessed we were to live in such a beautiful place.

CHAPTER TEN

A LETTER TO
THE IRISH TIMES

'Intolerance is itself a form of violence and
an obstacle to the growth of a true democratic spirit.'
Mahatma Gandhi

When discussing the book, Dad and I did debate long
and hard whether or not to include this chapter. It covers
things that are in the past and some things are better left
there, but we felt that it was important to show how Dad
felt about what was happening in Northern Ireland in the
late 1960s.

Dad left Northern Ireland for Zambia in 1966, a time
when the violence in Northern Ireland was increasing and
divisions amongst Catholics and Protestants were creating

a culture of violence, fear and intolerance. Dad has always loved Ireland and always loved the fact that rugby had a team that included players from the whole island of Ireland and, unlike football, it was not divided.

❀

'I am greatly saddened by the thousands of people who died in Northern Ireland as a result of the Troubles. During the Troubles when my friends in Zambia heard I was going home on leave and then they would hear the latest report of a bomb going off or yet another shooting, they used to say, "You're not going back to Belfast, are you?" I would shrug and wonder how to explain the necessary resilience that all Northern Irish people grew to have when living with the threat of violence every day.

'In 1966, I felt compelled to write to *The Irish Times* [the letter was also published in the *Belfast Telegraph* and the *Belfast News Letter*] from Chingola, about what I felt was the increasing level of intolerance and religious hatred being perpetrated at the time by the Reverend Ian Paisley. I also felt very sensitive about the fact that I had many friends from the Republic of Ireland and many liberal-minded friends in the North, and I wanted them to know that I in no way shared these views.

'The reason I raise the topic of this letter here is to show not only what I believe history will, in time, make of the Reverend Ian Paisley, but to show how strongly I felt about the spreading of hatred in a county I loved and was proud to call home.'

Anyone who spends any time with Dad will very quickly come to know that he has never judged any human being on their colour, creed or religion, and if he does judge anyone, it is on their character. Dad has never in his life been one to court controversy or to seek the limelight – in fact, quite the opposite – but he also abhors violence and intolerance and so, in this instance, his values caused him to speak up. More importantly, he wanted to make it known to his friends in both the North and South that he was totally opposed to the views that the Reverend Paisley and his followers were expressing at the time.

26 July 1966

Sir

Irishmen of all creeds in this part of Zambia have been saddened, dismayed and finally sickened at the recent happenings in Ulster, for the exploits of Mr Paisley and his followers have reached even this part of Africa.

The spirit of toleration and regard which has been growing in Ulster between Catholic and Protestant appears to have been shattered by the tragic events of the past months.

We have read that the Prime Minister Captain

O'Neill has finally had to denounce this man and his bigotry. Doubtless, he would have done so sooner, only he had no desire to make a martyr of Mr Paisley and probably felt that the man was hardly worthy of attention. He hoped I suppose, like many of us, that he would eventually disappear and his ideas with him. However there are times when the insignificance of the accuser is lost in the magnitude of his accusation and the evil he creates, and so Captain O'Neill has had to speak out against this man. One can only hope that all liberal minded Irishmen, especially Protestants in Ulster, will support the Prime Minister in his condemnation of this man and let Mr Paisley see that he hasn't the following that he claims.

In the eyes of his adherents Mr Paisley is already almost a martyr and I believe he has mentioned that he is ready to suffer like the martyrs of old for the cause of Ulster Protestantism. An old friend used to say somewhat cynically in speaking of the martyrs of bygone years, that some of them were so anxious for martyrdom that if they saw two faggots burning [faggot means a pile of sticks burning on the ground], they immediately jumped on the flames. Mr Paisley has been searching for his two faggots for a long time, and after his recent denouncing, may possibly be considered in some circles as the Saint Ian of Ulster. The martyrs of old suffered nobly in a cruel age for a worthy cause. Mr Paisley's talk of suffering is ludicrous, and his cause, religious intolerance, which inevitably brings with it hatred of neighbour, is just about the lowest for which anyone could suffer.

One wonders sadly what further harm he has to do, to add to this self-imposed and worthless martyrdom.

The late Adlai Stevenson in speaking of Eleanor Roosevelt shortly after her death, said 'she was always more ready to light a candle than to curse the darkness'. Mr Paisley has lit no candles of love, goodness, magnanimity or tolerance. He has spent his time and energies cursing what he considers to be darkness and unfortunately has managed to recruit followers to his creed.

Mr Paisley's 'darkness' however is not darkness to us all. Many of the finest, noblest and most likeable people I know are members of the Roman Catholic Church and I am glad to be able to call them friends. One does not have to live long in underdeveloped countries, whether in Asia or Africa, to see the magnificent and altruistic work done by priests, nuns and Roman Catholic lay people in hospitals, in all forms of service to the community, leper colonies and in education – to mention a few. To have to write such things should be entirely unnecessary – they are self-evident truths – but they have to be said to counteract the creed of those who believe they have a monopoly on the Christian religion, and that nothing *good can come from anything or anyone outside of their own narrow-minded and prejudiced ideas. What a pity the misdirected energies of Mr Paisley and his followers couldn't be used to build, like these people, instead of to destroy.*

Some time ago a minister from outside Ireland stated that he would never come back to speak in Ulster because the place was so full of 'spiritual night clubs', places where the 'religious' went along to be entertained and have their emotions stirred. Ulster is be-devilled by such religious clubs, where men like Mr Paisley entertain, making feeble and inane jokes, and obviously in some of these 'night clubs' stirring up the base emotions and religious intolerance, bigotry and hatred. The spiritual gain to the community resulting from such meetings is nil. Such 'entertainment' always seems to collect its followers. It reminds one of the verses:

> *The folk that live in our town,*
> *Their hearts are in their boots*
> *They all go to hell they do,*
> *Because the hooter hoots.*

Mr Paisley has hooted and the mob obediently falls in to fulfil his commands, without thinking of the consequences. One can almost hear in parts of Ulster the usual excuses for such deeds — we didn't start it, we are only answering them in their own fashion, for their past actions. Are we in Ulster so spiritually poor that we can only return violence with violence? Surely a so-called minister of religion could find a better solution than the fanning of the flames of hatred between neighbours?

Mr Paisley is considered by many to be a sincere man doing what he considers best for Ulster. There is no man more dangerous to a country or to a cause than the 'sincere man' who is wrong and whose sincerity is not combined with wisdom, intelligence and respect for the individual of whatever class, religion or colour. Mr Paisley is possibly displaying much sincerity but the latter qualities are sadly lacking. Do Mr Paisley and his followers really believe that the building of barriers between Catholic and Protestant and the formation of a religious apartheid is for the good of the province? What exactly are Mr Paisley and his followers trying to achieve? The fruits of their policy so far have resulted in riots and death. Would they like to massacre all Catholics, burn the chapels and have Ulster all to themselves? This is what Mr Paisley's roaring throughout the Ulster countryside would appear to suggest. Whatever would he do then? One hears he is not very keen on 'High Church' Anglicans.

All this nonsense he talks would, of course, be extremely humorous and Mr Paisley a good subject for cartoonists, if it wasn't for the fact that the seeds he is sowing create such evil and from them spring despicable actions. One can only hope that as few people as possible will be 'taken in' by this man's obsessional ravings and that all Irishmen will realise that he is a menace to the country.

As I write this letter, I am wondering if I was living in Ireland now, would I have the courage to post it? After the recent events in Ulster, I am doubtful. Some time ago a Protestant friend was striving to increase the harmony between Catholic and Protestant – word of this reached the ears of the staunch upholders of Ulster Protestantism – his home was subjected to day and night telephone calls for a month, many of them revolting. The culmination was a threat to the life of his wife, which forced him to ask for police protection. Such is the state of democracy in Ulster – freedom of thought, word and deed; so long as you think, speak and act according to the rules of the man who formed his own 'Free Church'.

Distance from Ireland in this instance does bring its compensations and so I post this letter.

Yours, etc.
41–7th Street, Chingola, Zambia

CHAPTER ELEVEN

HONOURS RECEIVED AND GIVING BACK

'Strive not to be a success, but rather to be of value.'
Albert Einstein

I once asked Dad how he would like to be remembered and he said that just being a decent human being counts for a lot and if he was remembered that way, it would be more than enough. For both his skill as a rugby player and his work as a surgeon in Zambia, Dad has won many awards, as well as having two honorary degrees. He was also awarded an OBE on 3 March 1959.

❀

'I was thrilled to receive both my honorary degrees. The one I received from Queen's in 1991 was very special to me, with it being where I studied to get my medical degree and also because it recognised my work as a surgeon in Zambia. I was also very proud to receive an honorary degree – a Doctor of Law – from University College Dublin in 2009 and I was in the very prestigious company of the great Brian Friel, who was awarded the Ulysses medal, and the late poet Dennis O'Driscoll.

'I was always very humbled to receive any recognition for my work as a surgeon, as this was my life's work and it meant a great deal to me. After my return from Africa, I was awarded the Silver Medal from the Royal College of Surgeons by the then president Barry O'Donnell. He wrote an excellent book on paediatric surgery that I referenced many times when out in Zambia, so it was a great honour to receive the award from him.

'On 31 January 2007, I was recognised for my medical work by the *Irish Journal of Medical Science* and the Royal Academy of Medicine in Ireland, where I was awarded the Lifetime Achievement Award at the Doctor Awards in Dublin. This award also had a lot of significance as it represents a lifetime of my work and to have that work acknowledged by your peers is very special indeed.'

'I could always tell those awards meant so much to you – if I remember rightly, you were also honoured by the Faculty of

Sports and Medicine of the Royal College of Surgeons Ireland. That was an important award too.'

'Yes, I received that in September 2007, they awarded me with an honorary fellowship which I was delighted to receive.

'I was also very humbled to have been awarded an Honorary Life Membership from the Royal Dublin Society. The RDS has a rich history and it is a real honour to be named alongside other honorary life members, including former presidents, Nobel laureates and others who have made a significant contribution to society.'

'We nearly forgot about your OBE. What did that feel like?'

'Oh, yes of course, I received that in 1959, the Queen asked me how long I had been playing in internationals. I said, "About ten or eleven years, but old age has crept up on me now", to which she laughed.'

There are too many rugby awards to mention them all and my brother Caleb and I have been the beneficiaries of some great nights out to celebrate Dad's achievements. In 2008, Dad was inducted into the International Rugby Board's Hall of Fame, but was unable to attend the event in London. Caleb received a call from Syd Millar to ask if we would be able to go to London to collect the award on Dad's behalf – I can tell you, Caleb and I did not have to be asked twice. We jumped at the chance. We flew to London in November for the awards ceremony. I remember our hotel looked out over the London Eye and the Christmas lights were on. It was all very festive and luxurious.

I can honestly say, I don't think I have ever been as star-struck in my life as I was that night at the ceremony. Everywhere I turned was another famous rugby player. From Dan Carter to Francois Pienaar and many others. Leaving the hotel to go to the awards ceremony, who jumped into our taxi but the great Gavin Hastings. We had a great night, but it was a shame that Dad couldn't be there to collect his award.

'You've also been inducted into several Halls of Fame, can you remember them all?'

'Well, I certainly remember the Texaco Hall of Fame award in Dublin in 1977, where I was the first rugby player to be given that honour. I also remember being inducted into the Rugby Writers Hall of Fame in 1991.'

Actually, speaking of that Texaco Hall of Fame award, I found this article entitled 'That Great Kyle Speech' from January 1978, where they actually reprinted the whole of your speech, which went:

'It is a wonderful and delightful pleasure to be here tonight. I remember once hearing a story about George Bernard Shaw at a party when an effusive hostess came up to him and said, 'Mr Shaw, are you enjoying yourself?' and he replied, 'Madam, it is the only thing

I am enjoying!' Might I assure you that in spite of this speech, this is for me one of the most remarkable occasions of my life.

Many years ago Ernest Hemingway said if as a young man you have been lucky enough to have lived in Paris then wherever you go for the rest of your life Paris stays with you, for Paris is a moveable feast. As a young man, I was fortunate to play rugby for Ireland – all my life, it has been a moveable feast and tonight the champagne has been added to that feast: to those who have added that champagne I am indeed grateful. To the Texaco people who inaugurated these awards, my grateful thanks and to those who chose me for this award, to be the first rugby player – and of this I am very deeply conscious – to enter the Hall of Fame, this is indeed a wonderful honour.

Those of us who are receiving individual awards like this, I think are tremendously conscious of the fact that we played on a team. I don't think I need to remind an Irish audience of the words of Yeats after he left the Dublin Municipal Gardens when he said:

Do not judge alone this book or that,
Come to this hallowed place
Where my friend's portraits hang and look thereon
Ireland's history in their lineaments trace,
Think where a man's glory most begins and ends
And say, my glory was I had such friends.

Perhaps 'glory' is too strong a word, but those of us who have played in any game are very conscious of the fact that the honours that we have received were made possible by other people who set the stage for us. For those hard-working, anonymous forwards who toiled and slaved on the rugby field and allowed the glamour boys in the three-quarters to run around and score the tries, I'm deeply conscious.

I read some time ago of a man who was a wonderful highboard diver. He could do back pikes and three and a half somersaults from magnificent high boards and everyone thought this was wonderful. The only problem was that when he hit the water his friends had to jump in and pull him out because he couldn't swim.

I think in a way three-quarters in rugby are a bit like that. Our friends were there pulling us out and toiling in order to allow us to exhibit ourselves.

One thing finally before closing. Might I just say what a tremendous enrichment is given to my life by the fact that I played for a side which represented the whole of Ireland. I know that I would have lost a tremendous lot if I had been playing for just one part of the country.

Looking back on those years and on the great pleasure that it always gave me to come down and play at Lansdowne Road, my favourite ground, to have made the numerous friends, to have indulged in

the delights of the game here and elsewhere and above
all, to have come back here to receive this honour in
Dublin tonight, I can only say thank you. It is a great
and lasting memory.

'Not a bad speech at all, Dad! We love it when you get awards,
as we get a good night out! Do you remember the RTÉ Sports
Awards a few years ago?'

'Yes, it was December 2011. I was also inducted into
their Hall of Fame. It was a very enjoyable night and very
good of Brian O'Driscoll to present me with my award.
I respect him enormously both as a player and a person –
but enough talk of awards now.'

When I sat down to talk to Dad about all his rugby
awards, he became a little self-conscious and said that while
it is lovely to receive the recognition, it sometimes seems
a little over the top to him. I found myself reminding him
that he brought a lot of pleasure to a lot of people through
his skill on the rugby field.

I do remember him looking a little uncomfortable once
at a ceremony in the Burlington Hotel where he was voted
Ireland's Greatest Ever Rugby Player. I ask him if I was
right about how he felt.

'Whilst it was lovely to be recognised in this way and I
don't wish to in any way denigrate the award, which I was
totally delighted to receive, what I am not very comfortable
with is being labelled or compared to other rugby players

and all the debates about who was the greatest. We played rugby in completely different eras. How can you compare two players who played with a completely different ball, a different set of rules and when one player played in the amateur era and one plays or played in the professional era? You may as well try and compare two different sports. I have learned now just to shrug my shoulders and take it for what it is – someone's opinion.

'One of the most fulfilling aspects of having enjoyed an international career and having a certain amount of notoriety is to have the opportunity to give something back. I have been very lucky to be involved in several charities, most notably The Wooden Spoon, of which Willie John McBride and I are co-presidents, and the Charitable Trust. Both do fantastic work, the former for a variety of causes and the latter raises money for injured rugby players. I was also made patron of the Neri Clinic, a charity set up in Dublin that raises funds to provide medicine and doctors for a clinic in Lusaka in Zambia – they do fantastic work and I am proud to be associated with it.

'One thing I won't do is accept money for talking at events, even though I am often offered it. If they insist on giving me money, I donate it to charities. Often I was given a token of their appreciation with some crystal or another present.'

'That is why your cupboards at home are creaking under the weight of different types of crystal!'

'Living and working in Zambia made us very aware how fortunate we were in comparison to those whose lives were so difficult. I witnessed so much poverty and death when I lived in Chingola and no matter what you give back, every small gesture of help or kindness unites us as humans and adds more meaning to our existence. Ireland is a very generous nation and it is heartening to see that we have not stopped giving to those less fortunate, despite our country's own issues.'

CHAPTER TWELVE

THE AMATEUR ERA OF RUGBY

'Two years before, I had gone to Penarth
with my father to watch Kyle play in the Barbarian
game. "Now there's a player that you ought to
be like," my father had said.'
Cliff Morgan

It is now over fifty years since Dad played rugby, so there would be something very wrong if the game hadn't evolved, but I am interested to hear whether he believes all these changes have been for the good of the game.

❁

'Rugby is a totally different game today from the game I played. For one thing, the ball is lighter and more dynamic. In my day, the ball was made of heavy leather and when it rained it became even heavier. Then, players often wore boots with steel toes and kicked with the point of the toe using a straight run towards the ball. Now they kick with the side of the foot.

The rules have changed completely as well, it is more of a kicking game now and the defences are so well organised that it has become much less of a running game, which I think is a shame. In our day, the ball came out of the scrum more quickly; nowadays it can be held up. Today, by the time the out-half gets the ball, the other team are lined up waiting. The days when the likes of Cliff Morgan, Barry John and Mike Gibson could cut through the defence are very few and far between.

'I remember Dickie Lloyd who played in 1910 giving me great advice about running rugby. He said that I only needed to be fast over a distance of twenty-five yards and that I should practise running at that speed. He also told me to carry the ball when I practised my sprints, and that was what I did. I ensured I was fast over twenty-five yards. Even in rugby boots, if you were a reasonable sprinter, you could probably go a hundred yards in say twelve seconds. So you are covering eight yards a second. If you could gain half a second on your opposite number, you could gain four yards on your opponent and you were through. That was where my ability was – to get the ball and take off like a bullet. I had that. It was one area I practised, and I also practised running sideways, also taking off on one foot

Side-stepping the opposition at Murrayfield, 1953.

and then the other. Aside from that, I was never in a gym or lifted weights in my life.

'It's not just the game that has changed, the players have too. When we went off on the Lions tour to New Zealand and Australia in 1950, there wasn't one player over fifteen and a half stone or over six feet two. Today, the lightest players are fifteen stone and the majority of the players are over six feet tall.

'As regards internationals, we rarely trained together as a team. For home internationals, we would take the early train down to Dublin on a Friday and have lunch in the Shelbourne Hotel. We might have a run out in Trinity College for forty-five minutes or so and then we would have a team talk where there was no coach, just the captain – though we didn't take the talks too seriously. I liked to lie in bed in the hotel on the Saturday morning of a game and enjoy bacon and eggs. I didn't eat lunch, as I felt it was too close to the game and I wanted to have all of my energy available to me.

'After the game, we dressed for dinner and had a meal with the opposite team. When we were in Dublin, there was a dance in the Metropole which went on until twelve o'clock. There was also a dance in Clerys which went on until one o'clock in the morning and if you still wanted more after that, you could go to Bective Rugby Club which went on until three o'clock in the morning. After that, you might be feeling a bit peckish and often a group of us would go to a restaurant in Dublin called The Green Rooster on O'Connell Street which was open all night.

'To find out if you had been selected for the next international, you listened to Radio Athlone on the Sunday evening, where they announced the team, as the selectors had chosen the side on the Sunday morning. So you didn't hear whether or not you had been picked for the next game before anyone else heard. Often my parents would listen if I was out at the time, and let me know if I had been selected or not.

'I remember when Paddy Reid turned to rugby league, the powers that be wanted to know if I would turn professional. Despite Paddy telling them there was no way I would, they were not deterred. I was on holiday in Portrush when they came to see me to try and persuade me to switch codes. I politely but firmly told them I was not interested.

'When Robin Thompson turned to league, in about 1956, after being captain of the Lions in South Africa in 1955, he was treated like a pariah by those involved in the union game. Robin's father had died when he was young, and his mother had worked all her life to give Robin and his brothers a good education and Robin wanted to be able to support himself and to give something back to his mother. He didn't tell her that he was going to change codes, as he knew she would try and talk him out of it. She was out one day and saw a headline in the paper: "Irish rugby international player turns professional." She wondered who it was and when she saw a man reading the *Belfast Telegraph* on the bus, asked him if he wouldn't mind telling her who the player was they were talking about. When he said Robin Thompson, she nearly fell off her seat. Mrs Thompson was incredibly upset about his decision.

'Ernie Crawford heard about this and he got in touch with Robin in England. He said he was going to sort it out and he acted as a mediator. He rang Mrs Thompson and put across his point that Robin should be allowed to make his own decisions and although she may not like it, she had to respect it, as Robin was trying to support himself.

He reminded her that life is much too short for families to be falling out, as Mrs Thompson had stopped talking to her son. He told her that Robin was going to call her at eight o'clock that night. Apparently Ernie said to Mrs Thompson, "Please remember that he is doing what he thinks is right. He needs your support at this time." After talking to Robin, she finally came around and accepted his decision.

'It was very difficult for Robin Thompson, he was asked to leave various rugby clubs. He told me that he walked up to friends and they turned their backs on him and walked away from him. Personally I think it was disgraceful, but it shows how strongly people felt about being loyal to rugby union, if that is where you had started playing rugby.

'In those days, you had to supply all of your own equipment. I met Rob Kearney's father before the 2009 Lions tour and he told me that each player was given eighty pieces of kit from clothes to boots, to bags to pens and everything you could ever need.

'In my day, rugby was played more for the huge camaraderie of the game and for the honour of playing for your country.

'I am so grateful for what rugby has given me throughout my life. I have made great friends and I am especially pleased to have friends from both North and South of Ireland. I have also travelled all over the world.

Since retiring in 2000 and returning to Northern Ireland, I have been overwhelmed by the kindness of the rugby world in inviting me to so many functions.

'The other thing I am very proud of is that Ireland plays as one nation and we were all happy to play as one nation. I was always happy to face the flag and to stand before the Irish anthem. I don't mean to be controversial at all, that is just how I personally felt.

'One area of the modern game that does concern me greatly is the number of concussions and injuries. Guys of fifteen or sixteen stone in weight are running straight at each other. If a player is concussed, he should be taken off the field of play immediately and not allowed to come back on. Brain injuries are very serious and the brain needs complete rest for a week or more if it has taken a knock. It has become an attitude of winning at all costs and this is a very narrow and dangerous development. It is sad to think that it took the death of a schoolboy and the work of the boy's father to highlight the problem and make it serious enough for the IRFU to do something about it. I appreciate that this subject is being talked more about now and that is a very good thing if it prevents players in the future becoming seriously damaged in the long term.

'With the money involved in rugby today, there is so much pressure on the players to do well. Every game is analysed afterwards, every move scrutinised and every mistake highlighted. It is of course natural that the game would develop and it had to develop, but sometimes I have to wonder if it has all gone slightly overboard, particularly when you hear of young boys taking various supplements. That is too much, in my opinion.

'I don't regret the fact that I played in the amateur era. I don't think I would have enjoyed playing in today's professional era.

'The game itself has lost some of its appeal for me, as it is now much more about running into your opposite number, whereas in my day you were trying to get around them or away from them as fast as possible. I think the modern game has led to far more injuries and we won't know the impact of that for at least another decade, but we are already starting to see more players suffering from the after-effects of so many blows to the head.

'In saying all of that, though, I don't wish to disparage the game in any way. It is the sport I will always love. It has developed for the better in many ways. Players are looked after very well and many go on to have a good career after their rugby-playing career. There is still a great camaraderie in the sport and I still enjoy watching the games.'

CHAPTER THIRTEEN

FAMOUS ENCOUNTERS

'Think like a wise man but communicate
in the language of the people.'
W.B. Yeats

As I drove through the Mourne countryside, looking up at the mix of purple, brown and green shades reflecting off the mountains, I thought about the parts of Dad's life that we have not yet discussed and what other surprising facts I might learn about him this weekend. As I reflected on all the places he has visited and the people he has met, I realised with a jolt that we hadn't yet talked about the many famous and interesting people he has met, many of whom may have influenced him in some way. After arriving and making a brew, I asked him to talk about some of the people he has met throughout his life.

❁

'Where should I begin? Well, there have been those people who I have met who have left their mark on me in some way, due to either their attitude to life or what they have achieved. I am very fortunate to say I have met some great men and women during my life. I remember when we were on the Lions tour to New Zealand, the team were privileged to meet several distinguished men. One of them was Captain Charles Upham who won two Victoria Crosses during the Second World War. He won one at Crete in May 1941 and at Ruweisat Ridge in Egypt in July 1942. He was one of only three people to win the Victoria Cross twice. He was a farmer in the North Island and Bill McKay, who had fought in the Burmese jungle, knew of him, so he asked the organising committee if it would be possible to arrange a meeting, and we were invited to lunch with him. It was a great honour and I remember him as a very quiet man.

'We also met Sir Bernard Freyberg, the Governor General of New Zealand, and he had also been awarded a Victoria Cross. He entertained us at Government House in Auckland. He was an inspirational soldier who had also been awarded the Croix de Guerre and the Légion d'Honneur. These are men who have shown extraordinary courage, the like of which we cannot even imagine.

'Returning home on the ship, when we docked in

Adelaide, we met Don Bradman, who was considered to be the world's most accomplished cricketer at the time. He was knighted for his services to cricket in 1949. The Lions were all delighted to meet him and we all had a great time chatting together.'

'I remember when you told me you had met Sean Connery at the 2005 Lions Tour in New Zealand. I was very envious.'

'Yes, it was quite funny. I introduced myself by saying, "Jack Kyle, from Ireland", and he replied with a cheeky grin, "Sean Connery, from Scotland." I had the pleasure of sitting beside his wife at dinner, a charming woman.

'Going back to talking about military men, someone who I would like to talk a bit about, and who had a great impact on me, is Lieutenant Colonel Robert Blair 'Paddy' Mayne. There is so much I could say about this remarkable man and I am only sorry that when I had the privilege of sharing a train compartment with him to Dublin from Belfast, I did not take the opportunity to talk to him. In saying that, he was known as a very shy man and was said to have found it hard to communicate at times.

'Blair Mayne was one of the highest decorated officers of the Second World War, who took over the SAS when the leader was captured. He won four DSOs [Distinguised Service Order], the Croix de Guerre and the Légion d'Honneur. He was also mentioned in dispatches and was known as the most loyal and brave soldier to have fought in the Second World War. He was an incredible man, who

Lieutenant Colonel Robert Blair Mayne, a most remarkable man.

led the SAS in some remarkable exploits. He seemed to be fearless. When he went on a raid he was exceptionally organised. Every single possibility was thought out. He was a popular leader with his men, who felt safe under his command. No man is painted in black or white and it is said that Mayne liked to read poetry, something else that adds to his complex character.

'As you know, Justine, he was an Ulsterman, born in Newtownards. At the end of the war, he came on to our Queen's Rugby Committee. He had played rugby for Ireland and had gone on the Lions tour to South Africa in 1938, a tour that was captained by Sammy Walker. The Merkel brothers who played for South Africa said that Mayne was the best forward they had ever seen play.

'When a person like Blair Mayne finds their true métier,

then they really become alive, and Mayne really became alive when he was fighting. Whilst there were many pacifists against the war, I believe that it was the lesser of two evils and there was no choice; Hitler had to be stopped. So Blair Mayne played his part in stopping this evil.

'This is one of the reasons that I like cowboy pictures. It is clear-cut. The baddies are dealt with and the goodies win! I also like the idea of total freedom that the cowboy pictures offer you. In life, we are never truly free. We are all bound by certain circumstances and commitments and I love to see the cowboy riding off into the sunset on his own!

'A couple of stories that illustrate the kind of person Blair Mayne was were told to me by Sammy Walker, who played rugby for Ireland and was a friend of Mayne. He told me Blair was the Irish Universities Amateur Heavyweight Boxing Champion in 1936. He was only twenty-three and was studying for a law degree at Queen's. Sammy had some amazing stories that he told me about him. Sammy and Blair had both been selected to play on the 1938 Lions tour. One night in the hotel room, Sammy heard this terrible racket out in the corridor. He went out to find Blair Mayne holding in his huge hands the head of Haig Smith [the assistant manager of the Lions tour]. He was pushing it up against the wall and shouting, "Who's a bloody Irishman?"

'Apparently Mayne had been out on the town and had

come back a little the worse for wear. Haig Smith had said to him, "Get to bed, you bloody Irishman."

'Sammy managed to intervene and got Mayne away from the manager and into his room. Haig Smith wanted to send him home. He was furious with Mayne and told Sammy that Mayne was a bloody nuisance and a threat to the tour, as they didn't know what he was going to do next. Sammy told me that the next morning when Blair had sobered up, Sammy went into his room and broke the bad news that the management were going to send him home. You have to remember that Blair was only twenty-three and still somewhat immature. He begged Sammy to help him and was practically in tears as he pleaded, "Don't let them send me home, Sammy, please don't let them send me home."

'Sammy, being the decent sort he was, felt sorry for his team-mate and perhaps some might say it was a foolhardy move, but Sammy went to management and begged them to let Blair stay and he promised that he would be responsible for Blair's behaviour for the rest of the tour. Management very reluctantly agreed and Blair got his reprieve. The fact that Mayne was also the best forward they had with them was obviously a factor.

'The other story that typifies the character of Blair Mayne happened on the rugby pitch. The Lions were playing against a tough provincial South African side and near the end of the game the South African forwards came away with the ball on their feet, as they did in those days, so what you had to do was to try and go down on the ball, throw yourself with your back to these guys, so your own forwards could come around. Sammy said that, as he was undertaking this, he received the most excruciating kick in the back. He told me the story like this: "It was so painful that I momentarily passed out. I came to very quickly and I lifted my head and I saw a couple of stretcher-bearers rushing onto the field. I thought, *Thank God, they've come to take me off.* I was more than a little surprised then to see them rush past me to a big South African forward who was lying on the ground completely out cold further along the field. The next moment, all I see is Blair Mayne towering over me saying; "Don't worry, Sammy, everything is under control!"

'Sammy told me he found out later that Blair had seen this South African forward put the boot into his back and being the great boxer he was, he grabbed this guy and delivered a six-inch upper cut and knocked the guy clean out. Blair was totally loyal to Sammy, and it was to be an indication of the total loyalty and courage that he would show as an officer in the war. The referee in the match went to Sammy and told him that if he hadn't seen the South African forward kicking him in the back, Mayne would have been sent off the field immediately.

'I admire that kind of courage and sheer determination, as well as the complete and utter loyalty Blair Mayne showed to his friend.

'Another event that influenced me, because it showed how determination and never giving up are so important, was the outcome of the last test match during that Lions tour. The Lions were losing the match 13–3 at half-time. This news went back to the UK and Ireland and everyone felt it was a done deal. However, the Lions turned the game around and they won 21–16. When the news went back on the radio that the Lions had won the match, the commentator who had heard the news thought there had been a mistake and reported that the Lions had lost the game 21–16 – later, he had to correct his mistake. There were eight Irishmen playing on that Lions side, a very impressive number in that era, men such as Harry McKibben, Sammy Walker, Blair Mayne and George Crummy. They were delighted to win the last test and I always thought it showed real determination and spirit, which I greatly admire.'

'I can see why you became so interested in him, he was quite a character,' I said, as we finished up for the afternoon.

Over dinner, we resumed our conversation about other people Dad has been influenced by and has had the good fortune to meet.

'One of the other men I would very much like to talk about is Frank Pantridge, who was a consultant physician at the Royal Victoria Hospital. I had the honour and pleasure of knowing him well and visiting him on several occasions. Frank studied medicine at Queen's and graduated just before the Second World War broke out. He joined up and was sent out to Malaya. He was captured by the Japanese and spent the rest of the war in captivity. The Japanese treated their prisoners very badly and Frank was incredibly lucky to survive. When the war ended and he was freed, he was about five stone in weight and very seriously malnourished. Frank witnessed some horrific things and it was said that he could hardly bear the sight of a Japanese person and you can understand why that was the case. He was awarded a Military Cross for his courage.

'He was a very bright guy. Northern Ireland had one of the highest rates of heart attacks in the UK. When you have a heart attack and your coronary arteries get blocked, your heart starts fibrillating, which means instead of beating at its normal rhythm, it starts beating at hundreds of beats per minute and then circulation is impaired, oxygen doesn't get to the brain and unless the heart is put back into normal rhythm again, the person will die. In Northern Ireland in the 1950s, they had a big defibrillator in the Royal Victoria Hospital. So when someone had a heart attack, the person would have to be brought by ambulance to be put on the large defibrillator.

'Frank Pantridge recognised that the important thing was to get the person defibrillated as quickly as possible, but sadly a high percentage of people died on the journey to the hospital. So he did two things. He realised they would have to get a portable defibrillator, so as soon as the patient started fibrillating, they could be treated in the ambulance. Frank, along with an engineer, set up a Cardiac Ambulance with what was known as the mobile coronary care unit, an ambulance with specialist equipment and staff to provide pre-hospital care.

'In 1965, he introduced his first portable defibrillator into an ambulance and, by 1968, the concept had been refined to a machine that weighed only three kilos and was very easy to carry. This transformed medicine and saved thousands of lives. The results of this were published in many medical and scientific journals, with the result that it was taken up by countries all over the world – except, surprisingly, the UK. It was very sad they did not have a portable defibrillator in every ambulance in the UK until 1990 and this both frustrated and saddened Frank greatly. Frank was honoured in many countries and he was given a CBE in 1979. It was an incredible contribution to medicine and today you will find a portable defibrillator in every train station, every airport, and every sports stadium in the world as well as in many other public places. When I think of Frank, I always think of the quote by John O'Leary, who said: "One man may honour a nation."

'Frank could be a very forthright person and did annoy certain people, but he was also very kind. When Noel and I were playing rugby, he would invite us out to the

Conway Hotel for a meal. For two impoverished students, as we were at the time, this was a real treat.

'One day in 2002, when Fred Anderson was back in Ireland and we went to visit Frank, he said to me out of the blue how he remembered me coming up to visit my mother back in 1955 when she was in hospital. I replied that he was correct and it had always been a bit of a puzzle to me, as she had died from kidney failure, following on from kidney disease, but the doctors didn't know what had caused it. I wondered had it been due to her last pregnancy.

'Pointing his finger at me as he had a habit of doing, Frank vehemently replied, "No. We didn't know it then, but we know it now; what killed her were the drugs she was given for her rheumatoid arthritis."

'I remember those were his exact words. The sadness of this was that the gold injections she was given were actually killing her. If they had stopped the injections, her kidneys might have recovered. She was only fifty when she died. I feel honoured to have known such a great man.

'I often reflect on those two men from Northern Ireland – Frank Pantridge and Blair Mayne – and wonder why Frank Pantridge was never given a knighthood, an injustice if ever there was one, and Blair Mayne was never given a Victoria Cross, although he was recommended for one by General Montgomery and by Stirling. I think the reason in both cases is they were controversial men and they had upset a lot of people who could have been responsible for getting them these honours. I often think people forget there is a difference between liking someone and respecting them for something they may have achieved in life. You may not like an individual, but it takes a wise person to be able to say whilst they may not like them, they can recognise their contribution to society and respect them for it. I think to not have fully recognised these two outstanding individuals for their huge contribution to society is a great shame.

'As my parents had always encouraged education and learning, I always found it a pleasure to meet people who were experts in their field, or who had a great intellect. I am thinking of people such as Conor Cruise O'Brien, who was a very stimulating person to be around, and also my old headmaster, Alec Foster. I have been very fortunate during my life to meet people such as this, who have enriched my life tremendously.'

CHAPTER FOURTEEN

A HEALTH SCARE

'Your attitude towards your health counts for a lot.'
Jack Kyle

While Dad and I were enjoying a beautiful spring morning out in his 'room with a view', I brought up the subject of Dad's health, as it has been a factor in his life in recent years.

❀

At the beginning of 2008, Dad kept coming down with colds that he never seemed able to shake off. He also began having the odd nose bleed and was just not feeling well. As Dad has enjoyed great health all of his life, it took him a couple of months to realise there was something seriously wrong. When he began to complain that he was off his food and felt very unwell, we all became very concerned. He visited his GP and had a series of tests done.

The results were not good news. He was diagnosed with stage four multiple myeloma, a cancer of the bone marrow. I am sure being a qualified doctor did not make hearing this news any easier – if anything, it probably made it harder. But at least Dad understood what he was dealing with, and he faced it courageously and never made a fuss, which is so typical of him.

I was devastated. He was taken into hospital the week of his diagnosis and his health rapidly deteriorated. The first couple of weeks were a blur of ongoing tests and all I can remember are a lot of consultants standing around his bed at the City Hospital, trying to decide what the next medical decision might be, to try and improve the situation. For a few weeks, the outlook was grim. Dad's kidneys weren't functioning properly, his haemoglobin had dropped to dangerously low levels and he could not eat, as the tumour that secreted the protein was causing him a lot of discomfort in his stomach. Following consultations and discussions, Dad's consultant, Dr Quinn, decided to give Dad a treatment known as plasma dialysis. This is a procedure where they take your blood out of your kidneys, clean it and put it back. It sounded altogether mad to me, but we were so desperate by that stage, I think we would have agreed to almost anything if we thought it would make the least difference.

'Do you remember that day, Dad, when you were given the plasma dialysis?'

'To be honest what I remember is how much better I began to feel after having it done. I hadn't been able to eat anything for several days and I remember finally feeling hungry and knowing that was a great sign.'

'I remember it so clearly, because we were so worried about you, especially as you couldn't eat anything. You were brought back from the dialysis and Aunty Brenda had come up to the hospital for a visit. After about half an hour of sitting with you as you lay listlessly in bed, you quietly announced that you were hungry and would like something to eat. Brenda and I nearly fell over ourselves in our haste to get you something. I remember when we left your room, we were just so damn relieved that you were finally showing signs of improvement.'

'From that moment on, my health did improve gradually and consistently. I had ongoing plasma dialysis and then just regular kidney dialysis for about a month, along with other treatments to boost my haemoglobin and also some radiotherapy.'

Dad was in hospital for about six weeks during April and some of May. I knew he would need looking after when he came out of hospital. As I was self-employed and my language classes would soon be over until September, I rearranged my schedule and gave up my English language teaching job that summer, so that I could move up north to care for Dad.

'I remember the day you came to take me home. I was really looking forward to my home comforts.'

'I never told you this, but I remember being pretty scared the day I was due to bring you home. Although you were so much better, to me you still seemed quite fragile. As we drove back to Bryansford, you chatted away and joked and laughed in the car and I felt like I was having an out of body experience. I didn't let on, of course, acting like this was all just another perfectly normal day, but inside I was both worried and delighted at the same time – delighted you were getting home, but worried that you would be all right and I would be able to look after you well enough.'

'I guess I didn't think much about anything except my relief at going home. It was great to have you staying with me though.'

Following extensive consultations with Dr Quinn and Dr Fogarty, Dad was told a drug called Velcade had been shown to have very good results on patients with multiple myeloma. He began a six-month course of Velcade, which fortunately did not have any of the side-effects of chemotherapy, so he did not lose his hair or feel sick. He was also put on a high dose of steroids, which pepped him up no end. On a couple of occasions, I had to come downstairs well after midnight and ask him to please turn down the music. Steroids can heighten your sensitivity and awareness to quite a degree, especially when you first start taking them.

'Do you remember that summer, how we sat out in

the back room and had our afternoon tea every day and chatted?'

'I remember I had the appetite of a horse because of all the steroids and we had a very relaxing time drinking tea and chatting about all sorts of things.'

I remember those few months with enormous gratitude – oddly, what should have been a terrible time, was a very special time for me. Dad and I spent hours chatting and I had the opportunity to say all I wanted to say and he did as well. He wrote me a special letter on my birthday in June, my most treasured possession, and I knew that no matter what happened in the future, I was exceptionally lucky to have had this time with him.

Every Monday morning, I would take Dad up to the hospital for his treatment and then bring him home again. I made him healthy shakes and as much healthy food as I could and did all I could to boost his energy levels. He showed remarkable resilience and would go for a very short walk each day, building up to a bit more as time went on. After a few months, I was standing at the kitchen sink one day and noticed a blur of colour flash past the window – I smiled as I realised it was Dad out doing his daily walk around the house and I was struck by his perseverance and how far he had come.

Aside from another short spell in hospital in October 2008 and in February 2014, Dad continues to live life to the fullest and I couldn't be more proud of him. I know the NHS comes in for a lot of criticism, but I must say I never saw a harder working group of doctors and nurses and I respect them enormously and needless to say Dad is very grateful to them.

It shouldn't take an illness to make you aware that spending time with a loved one is precious but sadly sometimes that is the case. I remember when Dad lived in Zambia, because we saw each other so infrequently, we always enjoyed each other's company and made the most of our time together. When you see someone all the time, you sometimes forget that we are just visiting this planet and being together is a great gift.

Dad is now eighty-eight years of age and is still receiving treatment for his multiple myeloma. He continues to enjoy life and though he is forced to slow down now, he still manages to attend the odd event and he is still independent. He is now supported and helped by medicine after dedicating his life to helping others with medicine, and whilst we would rather he didn't need it, it is reassuring to know that Dad's story is a cancer story of hope. Whilst there is ongoing medical research and continual advancements in the treatments for cancer, there is always hope.

CHAPTER FIFTEEN

THE GRAND SLAM IS FINALLY WON!

'Think where a man's glory most begins and ends
And say, my glory was I had such friends.'
W.B. Yeats

Growing up with two famous rugby players in the family, it is no surprise that most of my extended family are big rugby fans. My Uncle Noel's four daughters were all brought up around sport and spent many a Saturday at the Ormeau ground of North Rugby Club, as it was in the 1980s.

I remember the first time I became aware of the excitement rugby could generate. It was 1985 and my brother Caleb and I were both out in Zambia on our school holidays. Caleb and Dad had been listening to a rugby match on the radio as there was only one television channel in Zambia in those days and it only broadcast local programmes and a few American series like *Kojak*. I could hear the yells and shouts from Caleb from where I was sunbathing outside. I ran inside to see what all the commotion was about and Caleb said, 'We won, we won', while practically swinging my arm out of my socket. I remember thinking, *Jeepers, there must be something to this rugby game to get someone so excited.* So I decided to start watching. I picked a bad time. Ireland didn't win another Triple Crown until 2004. However, I became a loyal fan and have watched every single Six Nations tournament from that day to this.

I am interested to know how Dad felt about going to watch matches at the Aviva Stadium – though he still thinks of it as Lansdowne Road – after his rugby career had finished.

❀

'It is always very enjoyable going to support Ireland and especially when I can share the experience with either you or Caleb, and I even took Jack [Dad's grandson] to a game, which was great. It is always very interesting to watch a game that has changed so much. I think there is something special about rugby matches in Dublin, the atmosphere is always special, not just in the stadium but all around Dublin. I enjoy being in a hotel and meeting old friends. I also love going to the RDS in Dublin for lunch beforehand where you usually bump into someone you know.'

'I agree. I love the atmosphere in Dublin on the day of a Six Nations game. There's something electric in the air and the sense of anticipation is fantastic. I love the sense of camaraderie and the craic, not to mention the excitement of the game itself.'

Ireland had come close to winning the Grand Slam in the years leading up to 2009 and it seemed like everyone you talked to had the feeling this group of rugby players was something special. In 2009, there was expectancy around the Six Nations that was more than just hype. When Ireland went out and beat France comprehensively in their first match and then went on to beat England, we knew they meant business.

As the deciding match against Wales approached, I asked Dad who he was going to the match with. When

Watching Ireland win the Grand Slam with my son, Caleb, 2009.

he told me he had no plans to go and no ticket, I hoped someone would fix that and we would somehow be able to get Dad a ticket. Sure enough, Neil Hughes stepped up to the plate. Neil is a very good friend of my brother Caleb. He arranged not only tickets for Caleb and Dad, but laid on transport and by all accounts a five-star day was thoroughly enjoyed by all.

'It was a great day in the Millennium Stadium. It was also very special to go to such an important match with Caleb. The sense of excitement in the ground was overwhelming. Everyone was so kind, coming up and saying hello. We had a very enjoyable lunch before the game and Neil had organised everything so well. The game was a thrilling encounter and I don't think anyone could bear to watch when Stephen Jones took that final penalty

Congratulating Brian O'Driscoll after the Grand Slam win, 2009.

for Wales. We were all so elated at the final whistle. I was practically carried down to the touchline on a sea of people yelling and cheering. I remember Tommy Bowe coming over and I congratulated him and then I think he shouted to Brian O'Driscoll to come over. I had no idea that the photograph of my congratulating him would prove to be so popular, but it's a lovely memory for me to have and the whole day was fantastic. I honestly hope that Ireland can build on that success and we see more opportunities for Grand Slams in the future.'

While Dad and I are reminiscing about the 2009 Grand Slam, I am looking through all the press cuttings around that time, as Dad received a lot of press attention in the run-up to the final game against Wales and some in the aftermath. Two of my favourite pieces were Shane Hegarty's interview with Dad entitled 'A Pitch-Perfect Attitude to Life' and Dad receiving a mention in Ross O'Carroll Kelly's column in *The Irish Times*!

'Have you ever heard of Ross O'Carroll Kelly, Dad?'

'I know there is a column every Saturday in *The Irish Times*, but to be honest it's a bit lost on me.'

'Well, he's a satirical, fictional character based on a posh Dublin southsider, who is a a bit of an idiot and has delusions of grandeur as a former rugby player. As far as I'm concerned, forget about rugby fame, when you get a mention in a Ross O'Carroll Kelly column, you've really made it!'

CHAPTER SIXTEEN

LITERARY INTERESTS

'"Mother, hand me down the Burns!"
What my father frequently said to my mother.'
Jack Kyle

When chatting to Dad, you can be sure a line of poetry or a quotation from a famous writer is never going to be long in arriving, to illustrate a point or add poignancy to a story. As children, we used to groan whenever he would launch into a poem after dinner, but as an adult I have grown to love these times. On a visit up to his home in Bryansford, I asked Dad why he thought reading and literature have been so important to him throughout his life. 'I have always loved poetry and I think the reason I can quote so many poems is just the triumph of memory over creativity.'

I remember as a child the prolific number of bookshelves in our house in Zambia and what a source of fascination they were to me. I would look at the titles, not understanding what any of the books were about, but the smell, the covers and the newness or oldness of them, meant I spent a lot of time taking them off the shelves, flicking through them and putting them back.

I believe Dad could actually open a second-hand bookshop, so large is his collection of books. He has bookshelves in his study that go from ceiling to floor and go all the way round the room. He brought all his books back from Zambia with him and I could spend hours browsing through them. In fact, if I am ever looking for a particular book, before buying it, I go and see if I can find it in Dad's library!

I wondered if Dad's parents liked reading too.

❋

'Well, my father certainly did and I think my love of language and poetry partly came from him sharing poetry and stories with us. My father was a very intelligent man, who loved reading and knew how to express himself with eloquence. I can hear my father to this day saying to my mother, "Mother, hand me down the Burns", in reference to the great Robbie Burns. Every Saturday night, we had to sit through a reading of Burns and hours of poetry, including my father's favourite, 'The Cotter's Saturday Night'.

'On one occasion, my brother Eric arrived home to tell our father that he had to write a poem for the school magazine. My father could not resist having a go himself and he wrote the following poem, which was published in *The Owl* of the Belfast Royal Academy, the school magazine. This was a poem about the headmaster, Alec Foster, giving a talk about County Derry on the radio:

A short time ago we hadn't a care
The Head he decided to go on the air
Now the 'Dad' listening in was uplifted and merry
For sooth he was born in the County of Derry.

'Eric handed it in as his own poem for the school magazine but on reading it, the headmaster said, "Kyle, I think your father has had a hand in this."

'My father used to read Conan Doyle to me and Eric, along with another of his favourite writers, H. Rider Haggard. He encouraged us to always keep a dictionary nearby and to look up any words we didn't understand. This is a habit I have used all my life, and one which I hope I successfully passed on to you and your brother.

'As well as being an avid reader, I have managed – with the help of a few courses and a lot of discipline – to teach myself French. I am a total Francophile and on many mornings, I'll watch the news on French television. I love having my special satellite dish so I can watch all the French channels. In order to speak a language proficiently, you have to practise it continually, but you know that of course, being a French and Spanish speaker.

'I have always naturally gravitated towards people who shared my love of poetry and reading. Dai Gent, the reporter on the Lions tour, was one such friend. Dai had been a headmaster at a school in England and was then a reporter with *The Sunday Times*. When he retired from that, he was offered the job of rugby correspondent for the same paper, and, as I mentioned, he also played scrum-half for England in the early 1900s. I was very fond of him as he used to share books and poems with me. A month by ship from Liverpool to New Zealand is quite a long time to keep yourself amused, and Dai and I spent many an enjoyable night quoting poetry. I know that may sound very old-fashioned to some, but poetry is a universal language and I have always loved it.'

'What always amazes me though, Dad, is your capacity to remember such a variety of poems, which you can quote without a single need to pause and reflect or without making a mistake. I mean, you can probably quote over seventy poems off by heart and some of them are extremely long.'

'Well, for me poetry was the means to contemplate emotions that are sometimes difficult to express in thoughts and words. I often like to recite poetry to help me relax or even to get to sleep – I might l quote some Yeats or bits of a Shakespearean sonnet, to see if I can still remember it all.

'Another character on the tour to New Zealand was a Welshman known as Taffy Davies. He was a masseur for the New Zealand Rugby Union and he worked for the Lions as the team masseur and he also looked after the equipment. At sixty-two years of age, he was a very fit man. He quoted a poem, which Noel wrote down and I learned, and I can remember it to this day. Taffy told us how he found this poem which had been published by an Irish university student, who dropped out of university and became a taxi driver in Auckland. We tried to find out who the author was and to find a published version of it, but never succeeded. I also had a friend in New Zealand have a look for it in anthologies there, but to no avail. I know you searched for it online and could find no record of it either. It is a poem which in this day and age I feel all sportsmen would do well to remember, especially if they are becoming a little too proud of their achievements. Taffy would quote this poem if he felt that any of the team was becoming too arrogant. He would stand in the aisle of the team bus, throwing his arms in the air and reciting:

How frail the stay that holds up human fame
A mist, a breeze, a breath, a cloud, a name
Up like a rocket goes the gaudy flame
Down like a thunder bolt returns the same
Today on wings of welcome you may fly

And view a grateful country from the sky
Tomorrow heave a heavy bitter sigh
Midst plume plucked dreams of fortune sadly lie.
Today thy worshippers may kiss thy feet
Tomorrow drag thy body through the street.
Today midst fashion splendour you may dwell
Tomorrow languish in remorseless hell.
Today may drink oppression's bitterest cup
Tomorrow with the king of kings may sup.

'Never has this poem seemed more apt to me than in today's world of sport, where so many individuals are losing the run of themselves completely. In fact, all sportsmen and women would do well to remember it and place a copy somewhere as a reminder to them of what can happen in the world of sport.

'I remember on a wet and windy Saturday during the 1950s, I was playing a game of rugby at North Rugby Club, as it was known then [it is now Belfast Harlequins]. I cannot recall the game or the opponents. What I do remember are two remarkable people who were at that match, Louis MacNeice and Jack MacGowran. Jack was a superb actor, who had acted in many plays at the Gate Theatre in Dublin including *Waiting for Godot*, and I had also seen him act as the Dauphin in Shaw's *Saint Joan*.

'Mr MacGowran was prone to becoming rather overexcited at these matches and shouting encouragement from the sidelines. He had to be held back on several occasions from invading the pitch, by the much calmer Mr MacNeice, the well-respected Northern Irish poet.

'After the game, I was returning home in my father's car which I had borrowed for the day. I noticed Louis MacNeice standing at the corner outside the North Ground. I stopped and asked him if he would like a lift, which he gratefully accepted, and as I was a big fan of his I drove him, with a mixture of delight and nervousness, to Shaftesbury Square in Belfast where he was staying with his friends Mercy Hunter and George McCann. Mercy Hunter wrote an article about this meeting between Louis and I in a magazine which had the remarkable title of 'The Honest Ulsterman', and it was published in September 1983. It remains a great honour to me to this day, both that Louis was at the game and that I was able to assist him in getting to his destination.

'Louis was an avid rugby fan and during a radio interview when asked if he could make one wish, what it would be, he answered that he would like to play rugby like Jack Kyle. That meant a huge amount to me.

'In homage to him I recall 'Autumn Journal', one of my favourite poems of his:

September has come and I wake
And I think with joy how whatever, now or in future, the system

Nothing whatever can take
The people away, there will always be people
For friends or for lovers though perhaps
The conditions of love will be changed and its vices
   diminished.

'If I had a secret yearning for wanting to do something in another field, it would have been to play a musical instrument. I did play the piano for a time at university – but, playing cricket in the summer, rugby in the winter and trying to fit in my studies as well was too much, so I had to give up the piano and in time I also had to relinquish playing cricket.

'I always found it fascinating that many people who had succeeded in one field often had a yearning to have been successful in another field or career. Cliff Morgan told me a great story about Richard Burton. At a rugby match that Burton attended, he said to Cliff, "Ah, Cliff, if I could have played rugby for Wales, I would have given up playing Hamlet."

'I find this incredible, as I cannot understand how a man with the talent of Burton could, as he puts it, want to exchange his incredible acting talent for running around a field with a rugby ball.

'Another poet I had the pleasure to meet at a luncheon was Seamus Heaney. Following a talk that Seamus gave at the RDS in Dublin, I was sitting in the same row as

Seamus' wife Marie and was speaking to her after the talk was over. I mentioned how my father would often read poetry to us, including Robbie Burns. About a week later, I received a note from Marie with a poem that Seamus had written in the Burns idiom – there was also a little note from Seamus and he had signed it. Amongst the tributes paid to Seamus Heaney at his funeral, it was often mentioned that he was a kind and decent man, and I certainly agree with that.

'I remember when I was in Tahiti in the 1960s, I went to the island of Moorea for a picnic and swam in the beautiful water around that island. I hired a motorcycle and cycled around – and there was the most beautiful scenery in the more remote parts of the island. At one end of the island, I came across a house and over the entrance burned in wood were the words: "Robert Louis Stevenson lived here".

'Apparently Stevenson had lived there for a short time in the 1890s before he went to Samoa, where he died from a lung haemorrhage. The wonderful epitaph which he wrote is at his grave:

Under the wide and starry sky
Dig the grave and let me lie
Glad did I live and gladly die,
And I laid me down with a will.

This be the verse you 'grave for me:
Here he lies where he long'd to be;
Home is the sailor, home from the sea,
And the hunter home from the hill.

'I always took photographs on my travels and while I was taking a photo of the sign, an old man appeared and asked me if I was interested in Stevenson. The man lived in an old, very modest house overlooking this majestic view of the sea. He invited me in and told me he was a Dane, that he had been in the Danish Army before emigrating to America and worked in real estate. He made a lot of money for his employer, who gave him a large bonus of ten thousand dollars. I asked him what he was doing in Tahiti, to which he said, "It was a boyhood dream." He told me that he had married a Tahitian woman and with a twinkle in his eye repeated, "a dream, a nightmare, a dream, a nightmare". He said he had come to this house because he wanted to write something worthwhile and it was the right atmosphere to be inspired. When I asked him about the writing, he said that he wrote but realised it was not of any value and so he burned it. I remarked what a pity that was, to have burned his work, to which the Dane replied that when you have read a lot, you know when what you have written is not worthwhile. He then produced a scrapbook with various poems in it. He asked

me if I knew who had written the following sonnet, which
he quoted:

Since there is no help, come let us kiss and part
Nay, I have done, you get no more of me,
And I am glad, yea, glad, with all my heart,
That thus so cleanly I myself can free,
Shake hands for ever, cancel all our vows,
And when we meet at any time again
Be it not seen in either of our brows,
That we one jot of former love retain.
Now at this last gasp of Love's latest breath,
When, his pulse failing, Passion speechless lies,
When Faith is kneeling by his bed of death,
And innocence is closing up his eyes,
Now, if thou wouldst, when all have giv'n him over,
From death to life though might'st him yet recover.

'The Dane was particularly fond of this poignant sonnet
which I knew, but unfortunately could not remember
the poet. Before leaving, I took a photo of the Danish
man with his little granddaughter, who was about six.
He produced a card with his name and address on it and
asked me if I would send him a postcard when I got to the
"outside world". I cycled away and a hundred yards down
the road back to Papeete, I remembered that the author
was Michael Drayton. I thought about going back to tell

him but did not wish to disturb his siesta, which he had told me he was just about to take. I did send him a card and enclosed the photo of himself and his granddaughter.

'I often quote poetry during speeches. In Zambia, I was often asked to speak at various functions, including weddings, funerals and dinners. I did it because sometimes being in the middle of Africa, the parents of the bride or groom were unable to travel to the wedding. One particular event that I always remember was a wedding at which I was asked to propose the toast to the bride and groom. I had known them for a long time and they were great family friends. At the wedding, I quoted the following two lines of poetry by Conrad Aiken:

Music I heard with you was more than music,
And bread that I broke with you was more than bread.'

I had to smile at my own memory of those lines which Dad quoted at my own wedding too. *'But why do you remember that couple in particular?'*

'The reason I remember that couple so well is because they were hit by terrible tragedy later in their married life. The husband had a motorcycle accident and was paralysed and they got into debt paying his medical treatment and this led to further tragedy when his wife, despairing of the situation they were in, committed suicide. I always remember them with huge affection, because one Christmas evening in

Chingola when I was feeling a bit lonely, they called in for a drink and a chat and brought a stamp album for Caleb. At the wedding, I had not quoted the next two lines of the poem, because they are quite melancholic, but how apt they now seem: "Now that I am without you all is desolate, all that was once so beautiful is dead."

'A good friend of mine, Charlie Freer, who was Head of Sport for BBC Northern Ireland, introduced me to a cousin of his called Gareth Tyrrell and his wife Kit who lived in an old Georgian farmhouse in County Meath. Shirley and I often stayed with them on rugby international weekends after I had stopped playing rugby. Their house has a lovely friendly and hospitable atmosphere and they and their three children were always very welcoming.

'One Sunday morning we all went to the local Anglican Church at Trim. After the service, Gareth showed me a gravestone where the following was written:

I've had my share of pastime, and I've done my share of toil,
And life is short – the longest life a span;
I care not now to tarry for the corn or for the oil,
Or for wine that maketh glad the heart of man.
For good undone, and gifts misspent, and resolutions vain,
'Tis somewhat late to trouble, This I know –
I should live the same life over, if I had to live again;
And the chances are I go where most men go.

'The verse was engraved at the request of a young lad who had left the area, lived a full life and returned to die in the parish.

'Because the verse did not reflect the religious attitude of the time, it caused some controversy amongst the Parish Council, who were initially reluctant to allow the verse to be engraved on the headstone. However, eventually and generously, the wish was granted. I liked the poem very much and copied it down and later found out it was written by Adam Lindsay Gordon and was called the 'Sick Stockrider'. Gordon had emigrated to Australia and wrote most of his poetry there.

'I liked the poem because it expressed a certain attitude which could be criticised, as he had no regrets about the reckless life he had lived, but admired if taken another way, the accepting of the consequences of your actions. As I have always said to you and Caleb, if I felt you were on the verge of doing something that may lead you into trouble, "Take what you want, take it, but pay for it."'

As a parent, Dad used a mixture of literature, poetry and good old-fashioned common sense when trying to advise us on any matter. He gave us our freedom and his attitude was more that he was there if we needed him, and he would always do his best to help us, but we had to lead our own lives and make our own mistakes. With this in mind, he repeatedly told us that the sign of a mature individual is one who accepts responsibility for all of his actions. It took me a while to fully accept it, but it is as true as it ever was and will be, and it does take a certain amount of discipline to accept the part you have played in an event, rather than blaming someone else.

Dad is a great believer in poetry as a balm for all wounds and as a provider of encouragement to keep going. Whenever I went to Dad with a problem, I would be certain of one thing – there would be a quotation in there somewhere as a solution or to ease the pain. One of his favourite quotations came from Oscar Wilde which I heard so often I knew when it was coming, 'There are only two tragedies in life: one is not getting what you want, and the other is getting it.'

A poem he often recited and used in his own life when he was going through a difficult time, he passed on to me and at first I didn't really understand it, but after coming back to it later in life, I now see it as a very powerful poem for anyone facing a difficult time. It is 'To the Victor' by William Ellery Leonard.

> *Man's mind is larger than his brow of tears;*
> *This hour is not my all of time; this place*
> *my all of earth; nor this obscene disgrace*
> *my all of life; and thy complacent sneers*
> *Shall not pronounce my doom to my compeers*
> *While the hereafter lights me in the face,*
> *And from the Past, as from the mountains base,*
> *Rise, as I rise, the long tumultuous cheers.*

'I am so glad you shared that poem with me as it is has been really helpful to me in difficult times.'

'I found it to be so. Another poem I think is helpful if you feel you have done someone or something wrong, and you are tearing yourself apart with guilt, is Yeats' poem, 'A Dialogue of Self and Soul', especially the final verse:

I am content to follow to its source
Every event in action and in thought;
Measure the lot, forgive myself the lot!
When such as I cast out remorse
So great a sweetness flows into the breast
We must laugh and we must sing,
We are blest by everything,
Everything we look upon is blest.

'I also loved the poem 'Tears' by Lizette Woodworth Reese and I am a big admirer of Walt Whitman's series of poems, *Leaves of Grass*. I bought *Leaves of Grass* before a provincial game against Munster in Limerick and I adore the style of Whitman's poetry.

'I also came across some of the short poems of Walter Savage Landor recently, which I love because of their wistful nature:

Proud word, you never spoke,
But you shall speak
For not exempt from Pride some future day
Resting on one white hand
A warm wet cheek over my open volume you will say
This man loved me, then rise and trip away.

'He was buried in the English cemetery Piazzale Donatello in Florence, along with Elizabeth Barrett Browning, and I visited their tombstones when I was in Florence in the 1960s.

'A poem that your grandfather shared with me and which is definitely one of my favourites is Robert Service's 'The Shooting of Dan McGrew'. My father told me about how this poem was often staged at the old music halls at the end of show nights and it is so long, it could practically be a play. I can recite it in its entirety, and it goes on for at least ten verses. It's well worth a look if you don't know it. I especially love the first line: "A bunch of the boys were whooping it up in the Malamute saloon."'

'It reminds me of the other one you used to quote at parties, 'The Green Eye of the Little Yellow God' by John Milton Hayes, which begins: "There's a one-eyed yellow idol to the north of Kathmandu."

'Oh, yes, both good entertaining poems for quoting at parties!'

Some hours later when Dad has quoted from more

poems, he goes on to tell me about his love for the theatre.

'I remember the most amazing experience at the theatre I ever had. The audience sat mesmerised, not a sound coming from anyone. Siobhán McKenna had just finished playing Saint Joan in Dublin's Abbey Theatre and so spellbound was the audience that it took them a minute or two before they burst into rapturous applause. It was the greatest acting I ever witnessed.'

Music is another great love of Dad's life and he adores classical music. There was always a lot of music played in our house in Zambia, especially on a Sunday afternoon, when we would hear either classical or another piece of music, depending upon Dad's mood. He would often put on a piece of classical music and ask us who the composer was or which Beethoven symphony we were listening to. Beethoven's 'Symphony Number 5' was always a particular favourite. He also has a real love of jazz music. Louis Armstrong competed with Mozart, who competed with Billie Holiday. When they were younger, Dad and Uncle Eric also loved Glen Miller, Benny Goodman and Artie Shaw. Dad also loved some of the pop music of the time and liked to keep up with the latest trends in music. We used to have some great parties in Chingola and I can still remember as a child watching mesmerised while a load of adults gyrated round the floor to Rod Stewart's 'Do Ya Think I'm Sexy'!

Dad also has a wide range of books on philosophy and he likes nothing more than a good philosophical debate. He explains why one night over dinner.

'As you know, Justine, I am interested in philosophy and one of the major philosophical questions in life is the question of the lesser of two evils. Whilst it is important to try and take the right action in a given situation, sometimes you have no choice but to choose the lesser of two evils. It is wrong to get divorced, but it is also wrong to stay together if you are tearing apart the rest of your family and hurting people.

Another example would be a pacifist in the 1939 war who is against killing the enemy. What are the consequences of this? This means that if everyone thought like that, then Hitler would have won the war and the results of that do not bear thinking about. You have to say that in order to stop this evil, I have to kill Nazis. It is not right, but it is the only choice I have in order to stop the greater evil. Another example is the Americans dropping the bombs on Hiroshima and Nagasaki which caused the deaths of thousands upon thousands of people. It was an absolutely abhorrent act, but if they had not dropped those bombs and instead had invaded Japan, then at least half a million Americans would have been killed and millions of Japanese would have been killed because the Japanese would never have surrendered. There is no right answer in this situation but for the

Americans, it was the lesser of two evils. It also meant that many were liberated from Japanese prisoner of war camps. Whilst I am not for one second saying there was anything whatsoever that was good about the decision, sometimes difficult decisions have to be made. It is a grim reality of life.'

'*Yes, I just wish, as I am sure most people do, that these wars could have somehow been prevented in the first place, but that is a waste of energy. I see your point though, sometimes neither choice is a good one, but you have to try and decide which is the best option you have before you.*'

'The point being sometimes you have to take action even if it is not easy.'

I asked Dad what the best bit of advice that he had

Looking at photographs with Justine, 2014.

ever been given was. Although he admitted it was a hard one, he said it was probably the one piece of advice that he had passed along to us – that perseverance is the key to success. 'If you want to be good at something, you have to persevere no matter what.' He repeatedly told me that if you feel very strongly about achieving something, you shouldn't give up on it.

'In 2010 when the BBC asked me to return to Zambia to film the programme *Season Ticket*, Thomas Kane, the interviewer, asked me how I would sum up my life. I said I would feel incredible gratitude for the enjoyable and interesting life I have had, and I have also been incredibly lucky to have had a life of good health with very few injuries. As I mentioned in the letter to Cliff Morgan, I would use the words I learned from that priest in Clongowes one Sunday morning: "Look on the past with gratitude, the present with enthusiasm and look to the future with confidence."'

JACK KYLE'S
INTERNATIONAL RECORD

v. Australia, 1948, 1958

v. England, 1947, 1948, 1949, 1950, 1951, 1952, 1953, 1955,
    1956, 1957, 1958

v. France, 1947, 1948, 1947, 1950, 1951, 1952, 1953, 1954,
    1955, 1956, 1957

v. New Zealand, 1954

v. Scotland, 1947, 1948, 1949, 1950, 1951, 1952, 1953, 1956,
    1957, 1958

v. South Africa, 1952

v. Wales, 1947, 1948, 1949, 1950, 1951, 1952, 1953, 1955, 1956,
    1957

Being chaired off by Noel and Ronnie Kavanagh after my
forty-fifth cap, 1958.

ACKNOWLEDGEMENTS

Dad and I would like to express our gratitude to the following people:

- To Claire Rourke for your unending patience, kindness and skilful editing.
- To Ciara Doorley, and all the hard-working team at Hachette Book Group Ireland.
- To my cousin Lynne McGowan for providing the family information on previous generations and also to your neighbour Bill McAfee for bringing it to your attention!
- To my cousin Jan Gough, thanks for your generosity in sharing the many family photos. I would also like to thank the Henderson family for permission to use the photos Noel took on the 1950 Lions tour.
- To Roger Anderson and Jan Gough, many thanks for reading the manuscript and providing valuable feedback.
- To the extended Kyle family, thank you for being such a loving supportive family.

- To Caleb and Fiona, thank you so much for your encouragement and support.
- To Jack, Calum and Erin – we hope you will enjoy reading about your granddad's life, and in future years your children may like to read about their great-grandfather. Thank you for all the joy you bring to our lives.
- I would like to thank my husband Conor for encouraging me all the way and for providing invaluable feedback on the manuscript.

Finally, and personally, to Dad. Working on this project with you has been a complete joy. I would never have undertaken it without your faith in me and your constant support, which has meant so much. Thank you for everything.

Justine Kyle McGrath

PERMISSION
ACKNOWLEDGEMENTS

The author and publisher would like to thank the following for allowing the use of their copyrighted material in *Conversations with my Father*:

- All family photographs to the Kyle family
- All photographs from the 1950 Lions tour, used by kind permission of Andrew Henderson and the extended Henderson family
- page xiii: Albert Fenton
- page 22: © Radharc Images/Alamy
- page 25: Eric Kyle
- pages 34, 36, 47, 103 and 237: © REX/Daily Mail
- pages 54, 60 and 128: © Getty Images
- page 203: Mary McDonald
- page 212: Les Faber
- page 264: © INPHO/Morgan Treacy Alamy
- page 287: PA Images

- 'Autumn Journal' by Louis MacNeice reprinted by kind permission of Faber and Faber Ltd
- 'Music I Heard' by Conrad Aiken reprinted by kind permission of the poet's estate

The author and publisher have endeavoured to contact all copyright holders. If any images used in this book have been reproduced without permission, we would like to rectify this in future editions and encourage owners of copyright material used but not acknowledged to contact us.

INDEX

READING IS SO MUCH MORE than the act of moving from page to page. It's the exploration of new worlds; the pursuit of adventure; the forging of friendships; the breaking of hearts; and the chance to begin to live through a new story each time the first sentence is devoured.

We at Hachette Ireland are very passionate about what we read, and what we publish. And we'd love to hear what you think about our books.

If you'd like to let us know, or to find out more about us and our titles, please visit www.hachette.ie or our Facebook page www.facebook.com/hachetteireland, or follow us on Twitter @HachetteIre.